Disclaimer

References and quotation marks indicate when I'm using or distilling information from reputable sources. I try very hard to maintain high integrity of sources. Unreferenced comments are my opinion, either from experience or considering others' thoughts. I have tried specifically to avoid notes from Harvard and MIT course material and other copyrighted material.

Image Credits

Cover composition: Copyright © Dorian Scott Cole, all rights reserved.

Cover Image:

Kevin Dooley at Flickr.
https://www.flickr.com/photos/pagedooley/6861256042

Creative Commons license: Attribution 2.0 Generic (CC BY 2.0): Attribution and image change required to be noted.

Image was cropped to fit the cover properly.

https://creativecommons.org/licenses/by/2.0/

Preparing For The future of Work, Education, and Economy

AIP Initiative: Adapt, Innovate, Prepare

Mission: Help communities to be included in the economy and address related problems, through educational preparedness, business adaptability and recruitment, and well rounded continuing education.

Dorian Scott Cole, CEO

TechGenie Media, LLC

Vision: Excellent jobs, wages, and education for everyone

Instilling confidence to move ahead in education

Engaging curiosity to dig deeper

Stirring the soul to greater things
Adaptability to new jobs through education
Building a greater community for all

Copyright and Cataloging

ISBN: 9798653309519

Cataloging information
Preparing For The future of Work, Education, Economy
1. Cole, Dorian Scott, 1947 -
2. Nonfiction, economics, education

ebook available

See cover credits and copyrights on the next page.

Dedication

This work is dedicated to people who work hard to earn a living, who shoot for rewarding careers and good homes.

Acknowledgments

Grateful appreciation to my wife, Sheila, who sacrifices so that I can write, and who is my beta reader and strictest critic.

CONTENTS

CHAPTER 1: Why? The ever-changing American job landscape

Six-million years ago people invented beds and pillows.[i] It might have been fifteen-million years earlier, but the statistics are a bit difficult to dig up. Someone probably made a career out of making beds, and then hired others. It's the first known use of technology, but not the world's oldest business. Work changes are always about technology.

Technology changes everything including a good nights sleep, sometimes to a poor night's sleep as we worry about the future. It creates new products that improve our lives and work. It enhances manufacturing to improve productivity, meaning less labor. It creates new medical treatments. It also destroys many jobs. It moves relentlessly toward the future.

What does this mean for our future work? It's complicated. Understanding what is changing and why, is required to understand, adapt, innovate, and prepare for the next fifteen years.

> Job changes are an evolving area. Various factors can impact what is happening, including recessions, lag time in technology deployment, and experience. This is a cautionary statement. Some statements may seem contradictory. Being forewarned is forearmed.

The pace of change

The pace of change since that time when the beds and pillows were invented has steadily picked up pace, so that technology drives change faster and faster, building on itself. It's exponential–the pace of change chart line is going nearly straight up[ii]. And not only do things change very fast, we have to adapt very fast, and even our social leanings change. Surprise! We are now solidly in our

Fourth Industrial Revolution[iii]. It's digital. The ground is shifting again.

Whether we're stitching together beds or computer code, our jobs are likely to change for the better. More of them will be less monotonous or won't require as much manual labor*. Manual labor and disease are killers. People in the 20th Century when Social Security was created, were only expected to live 60 years on average. Technology has extended life expectancy to 78 years, and most people–the mathematical mode–will live to at least age 86, although obesity is now reducing this.

> *A substantial number of people want boring jobs. Supporting their families is their only objective. Additional education, training, and responsibility is often seen as an unwanted or even unattainable burden. Shaping the future has to be done with care.

The downside of this change is that as jobs are displaced by technology, there is no one-to-one job replacement. The person holding the job that's getting replaced will either have to get retrained or lose employment. People entering the job market need to know these new skills, or they won't get hired.

> According to Georgetown University's Center on Education and the Workforce, 99% of all new jobs created since the Great Recession require some formal education beyond high school.

Education hasn't kept up

"Fifty years ago, the U.S. had the best-educated workforce in the world. But we've been backsliding while other countries have zoomed ahead of us." "The result is that millennial workers in the U.S. are now tied for the lowest level of basic skills in the industrialized world," Tucker and Betsy Brown Ruzzi wrote in a policy brief "Message to America.[iv]"

College may not be the answer. Education will be fully addressed in later chapters.

What is changing, and is it important?

Automation has historically brought us major benefits. For example, As automation frees our time, it increases the scope of what is possible, we invent new products, new ideas, new services that command our attention, occupy our time and spur consumption, and those irritating Fidget Spinners.

People who are displaced move on to other jobs, often within the same organization. In the early days of the US, people were mostly tied to food production. Change has been revolutionary. Farming still feeds the world, but it went from 40% of jobs in 1900 to just 11% today. Manufacturing went from 32% to just 7% in 2020, losing 4% in 20 years.

People are now occupied in businesses that hardly existed a century ago, such as health and medicine, finance and insurance, electronics and computing, and credit counseling. Technology creates jobs while displacing others.

Technological change displaces people. Those displaced need to be prepared and have help to change to new jobs, or the displacement is devastating. The US Rust Belt cities are testimony to the devastation caused by technological change and outsourcing. We need to bring back rust.

 Communities also need to guard against widespread job loss that destroys entire communities. This can be prevented by diversification, so that wiping out a type of industry doesn't eliminate all jobs.

Sometimes gains are wasted. In the US and other Western countries, as companies gain efficiency, the gains go to the top 1% and don't help people very much.

In many developing countries, companies, employees, business clients, and consumers tend to be exclusive trading circles so that the economic benefit and opportunities never reach the wider population. It's imperative that we maximize the benefit to all of us, not just the privileged.

Being forewarned provides time and opportunity to address coming changes in constructive ways that prevent devastation of jobs, homes, and communities. The book *Our Towns*[v] provides examples of communities who were devastated by employers leaving. To recover they used various ways to improve work force education, diversify the types of employment in the area, make their communities attractive, and include new industries in guiding their education and workforce development.

Service jobs

We are now primarily a service economy (80%). We used to be an industrial economy producing goods. Now we provide services rather than goods. Technology makes us more proficient at some of our jobs, such as providing reporting and analytic tools for managers and accountants. For some it does away with their jobs, such as legal researchers whose tasks can be done by computer algorithms, and radiologists whose jobs can be done by computer programs.

Many retail stores are being eliminated by online companies like Amazon. Clerks at store checkouts are only needed for special circumstances. But at the same time, Amazon has created a large number of warehouse and other jobs. Walmart created new services, such as ordering items from online expanded inventories, and ordering groceries online with delivery to homes or waiting automobiles. Creating new jobs while replacing older ones has been the consistent history of technology.

Construction and maintenance

Construction and maintenance aren't likely to have major changes. We need houses and highways built, cars repaired, and sewers and songs unplugged.

Manufacturing

Manufacturing is only 12% of the economy, and employs only 9% of the workforce. Most jobs have been eliminated by technology or exported to countries with lower wages. Manufacturing jobs are targeted for more technological innovation. But someone has to program, oversee, and repair the robots.

> A lot of jobs will be displaced. The lower and higher the person's educational level, the more likely their job will change. In the past people could go to cities to find jobs. Those jobs now require more education and are out of reach for those without post-secondary education.

The Gig economy

Twenty-five percent of workers participate in the "gig" economy. Some estimate the number at 36%. It is growing. They are freelancers who have the expertise to do jobs, and work under contract. These jobs are temporary and flexible.

Companies love gig employees because they can avoid hiring full time employees for short-term projects, and they don't have to provide benefits, which is usually an additional 30% of wages. Workers often love them because they provide flexibility. Some are more permanent as in the Uber or Lyft type driver jobs. For some it's a second job used to support their families. Around ten percent of workers in the US use gig jobs as their full time job.

The difficulty with gig jobs is that there is no job security, and commonly no benefits. This means that when the job ends it may be months before they find another gig job. And no benefits such as medical insurance.

Another difficulty is that some contract supplier companies will make the lions share of the money, and give scant wages to those they hire. Sometimes this goes as deep as three levels, giving poverty wages and no benefits to employees.

Job types that will change over the next fifteen years

Brookings Institute findings are that "almost no occupation will be unaffected by technological change in the AI era.[vi]" There is a distinct indicator of which jobs are likely to change, across all job types. Jobs that are repetitive and don't require human judgment or interaction are likely to be automated. This includes legal researchers, radiologists, and people who put widgets together.

"Some of the most vulnerable jobs are those in office administration, production, transportation, and food preparation. Such jobs are deemed "high risk" with over 70 percent of their tasks potentially automatable. All of these either involve routine, physical labor or information collection and processing activities.

"High risk" jobs represent only one-quarter of all jobs, however, in places like St. Louis and Kansas City, nearly 50% of jobs may be affected. The remaining, more secure jobs include a broader array of occupations ranging from professional and technical roles with high educational requirements to low-paying personal care and domestic service work characterized by non-routine or abstract activities and social and emotional intelligence."

When it comes to AI (not robotics), a new report from Stanford and Brookings Institute, developed by using AI techniques, indicates that, "White-collar jobs (better-paid professionals with bachelor's degrees) along with production workers may be most susceptible to AI's spread into the economy." And, "... graduate or professional degrees will be almost four times as exposed to AI as workers with just a high school degree. Holders of bachelor's degrees will be the most exposed by education level, more than five times as exposed to AI than workers with just a high school degree."[vii]

Employment and Demographic Shifts

The employment shifts coming are: more physical jobs will be
replaced by robotics, and more intellectual jobs will be displaced
or replaced by AI, up to a total of 30% of US jobs.

The demographic shifts will include fewer people without degrees
going to the city for work, because the work there generally tends
to require post-secondary education. And workers in the city
leaving because they are replaced by AI, cities are too expensive to
live in, and the quality of life is affected by very long commutes,
high housing expenses, and susceptibility to pandemics.

Life in rural areas with cities under 100,000 people is becoming
much more attractive to city workers. The problem is, the jobs
aren't yet there. Generally where certain types of jobs are common,
there is a large nucleus of companies doing similar work, so people
with those talents are attracted to those areas. Silicon Valley is one
example.

Working from home may eliminate the problem of city location.
Home can be anywhere in the world.

An important shift making a demographic shift possible

People have been working more from home for the last thirty
years. The Covid-19 pandemic sent most employees home to work.
Without the commute and other complications, workers can be
13% more effective.[viii] Facebook and Twitter have decided most
employees can work from home, but perhaps with a cut in pay.[ix]
An IBM survey found that fifty-four percent of employees want to
work from home. Happiness with their work often increases by
22%. Happier employees stay longer.[x]

A Blind anonymous survey found that two-thirds of tech workers
would leave San Francisco permanently if they could work from
home.[xi] The tech field is aching for new places to live without all of
the headaches of large cities.

Companies may need the space given up by those who work from home. Social distancing is causing companies to rethink office strategies that group people together. Six feet spacing and barriers will make major changes to office layouts. And overall companies may have to lease less office space if half their employees work from home.

New forms of AI driven compliance may also come into being, supplementing current forms of monitoring, such as monitoring time on computers and phone. Generally most people want to do really good work and be productive, so you don't have to worry about them. Around 10% excel above others. But around 10% of employees continuously fall short of goals.

This has been my experience in managing field organizations where employees are not monitored and live in other states from the office. But it depends a lot on worker attitude. A culture of noncompliance can also be the downfall of an organization. I personally have worked from home fully, or at least part of the time since 1980.

Markets and the economy are also changing

The US population stopped its population growth phase in 2007. Europe stopped decades earlier. With the lack of population growth, markets won't grow much. This means companies have to get their profits elsewhere, like from saving on wages and jobs, or from selling more to developing countries.

Much of technology has peaked, so new products and product improvements on many products that used to drive manufacturing won't be coming. For example, consumer electronics will see very little technological change. Profits will have to come from elsewhere.

Medical and technology innovation are two large areas of future growth. STEM, Healthcare Professions, Healthcare Support, and Community Services will be the fastest growing occupations, but also will require high levels of post-secondary education.[xii]

In studies, people aren't wanting more and more of more and more. Consumerism is cooling.[xiii] And Millennials either want a different lifestyle or are simply too broke to buy things. Profits have to come from elsewhere. The economy, while stabilized by everyday costs of living, actually runs on consumer discretionary spending[xiv], which is money people can spend freely. This currently is soft.

> Salaries for the lower half of the economic scale not improving much, their personal credit debt is at record and potentially unsustainable levels eroding their discretionary funds, and they are the main discretionary spenders, profits have to come from elsewhere. Otherwise without these components to the market, we can go back into recession.

The economy has grown at only an average 2% annual rate since the Great Recession[xv], with around 2% inflation, and it has been a long period of growth with stock market corrections needed. "Roughly half the nation's business economists think the U.S. economy will slip into recession by the end of next year, and three-

fourths envision such a downturn beginning by the end of 2021."[xvi]
This is driven by the US economy and the world economy, which
is struggling. Companies retreat from hiring during uncertain
economic times. The impact of the recession started by Covid-19
isn't yet known.

Unlike the era following WWII, the markets are not going to drive
the economy, jobs, and wages to the extent they once did.

Regional impact

For a county or region, this means that the 35% of people who
only have high school diplomas, their jobs are likely at risk in the
long-term. This kind of widespread job loss will have major
implications for those family's economic viability, medical care,
and retirement. It can add substantial need for government
benefits. It can erode the area tax base while adding benefit
burdens. These are the economic conditions of Louisiana and
Mississippi, the poorest States in the US with the highest
dependencies on government benefits.

Some areas, like St. Louis and Kansas City[xvii] are likely to have
half of their jobs affected by automation. Major educational
assistance will be needed to keep people in the workforce.

Additionally, those areas most affected by a loss of jobs to
imports, experience lower rates of marriage and fertility, and drift
from supporting moderate to more extremist political candidates in
congressional and presidential elections.[xviii]

World leaders express the worry that persistence of this
gaping economic divide will do more than just limit
economic growth; it could even threaten the future of our
democracy, just as extreme inequality has done in other
countries in years past.[xix]

The US Middle Financial Class has hollowed out, leaving our
income across our population looking like a barbell, with half the
population on the low end, and half on the high end. Those with

the education and training employers look for, do very well economically. Those who lack that skill and education sink to the bottom.

Half of US households don't pay Federal Income Tax. Most of them draw government benefits, such as EITC.

While raising yourself up the stairs by your shoestrings may be an American value, many people are providentially hindered from improving their chances in the economy. It's up to the rest of us to help them find a way up. We all benefit with a better economy and less need for assistance if we do.

Short term job outlook – two years out 2019

For a look at the very short term, Georgetown University found in their study: *Job Growth and Education Requirements Through 2020*[xx].

- **Job Openings:** There will be 55 million job openings in the economy through 2020: 24 million openings from newly created jobs and 31 million openings due to baby boom retirements.
  [Note: 304,000 people retire each month. The number of new jobs created runs around 164,000 a month. Each year the aggregate number of jobs increases by around .33%.]

- **Education:** 35 percent of the job openings will require at least a bachelor's degree, 30 percent of the job openings will require some college or an associate's degree, and **36 percent of the job openings will *not* require education beyond high school [short term].**

- **Fastest growing job areas:** STEM*, Healthcare Professions, Healthcare Support, and Community Services will be the fastest growing occupations, but also will require high levels of post-secondary education.

- **Skills:** Employers will seek cognitive skills such as communication and analytics from job applicants rather than physical skills traditionally associated with manufacturing.

* STEM: BLS.gov defines STEM jobs as careers where "workers use their knowledge of science, technology, engineering, or math to try to understand how the world works and to solve problems."

Chapter 2: What can we expect from government

While it could be good for government to become involved, government has been very reluctant to become involved in economic, employment, and education affairs, except to exploit issues for their own gain.

The last government major involvement was the State Governors coming up with standards to teach for future workers. It turned into teaching to the test, and everyone hated it. Yet government controls educational standards and granting of degrees.

Trust in the US Government has been a 40 year slide, now standing at 17%[xxi]. The Congressional approval rating is identical: 17%[xxii]. In recent decades government has steadily decreased funding of higher education institutions, helping to send educational costs sky high, while sending more money to war and to debt interest. In local communities a promising program gets a good start, then the next administration is fundamentally opposed and cancels it. Government has proven over the decades to be unreliable as a funding partner.

> Currently politicians seem to follow the US Chamber of Commerce idea of rejecting anything that places any demand on the privileged role of business. Government is generally opposed to minimum wage increases, and in some areas even undermines or negates citizen ballot referendums. Issues with very high popular support are systematically ignore.

The poor reputation of government for ignoring citizens is richly deserved. As shown by a Princeton and Northwestern University study[xxiii] over a 20 year period, what citizens want has hardly any affect on legislation. "The public is often thwarted through inaction," The authors state, "The wealthy and partisan extremists often succeed at stopping proposals that are popular." They branded the US an "Oligarchy" rather than a Democracy. Representative government now primarily serves special interest lobbying. The recent election of a "bomb president," to clean out the government appears to have backfired. Expectations of a government role in anything appears dismal.

What can we expect from employers?

People haven't had much confidence in business or government to be responsive to people for decades. But there is possible change in the air.

Why are we in this position? It isn't your granddad's workplace anymore. Technological innovation and markets grew wildly after WWII, and employment and wages were great. Families thrived. Employees stayed loyal to companies, and companies stuck around so that people could retire from them. Employees and even the community were regarded by the business as stakeholders (having a stake in the company). Investors grazed on stock dividends rather than rises in stock prices.

Several things changed that work against jobs and wages. It's changes allowed by system[xxiv], so no one is at fault. The business of business is making money, and it has no other defined obligations no matter how much people would like to think it does, except regulations.

Previously as productivity (quantity made per hour, efficiency) rose, so did wages. Then in the 1960s productivity began to follow technological innovation in production rather than employee hours, so by the 1970s employee wages no longer followed productivity. As real wages flatlined, household income was buoyed by two incomes, compensating for the lack of real wage* growth.[xxv] Wage gains only went to the better educated.

 * There is a battle every year between wages and inflation. Inflation erodes the spending power of money. Real wages is the actual spending power of money. It's changed hardly any

since 1970, and for people in the lower half of the income scale, it's gone down.

Companies began acquiring their competitors for their technology and markets, and fired the employees. By the mid-1990s, "Merger Mania" became the name of the game, and it has continued to this day. Corporations also found they could export their work and supply chain needs to other countries with much lower wages, and this had profound negative impact on jobs and wages.

Companies also restructured and eliminated tiers of middle management positions. They passed off former manager responsibilities to hourly employees and repositioned them as "exempt status" (management, not hourly) employees with no wage increase. Corporations are net job destroyers.[xxvi],[xxvii] They eliminate more jobs than they create.

The impact of these several decades of change on people's wages, for the bottom half of income earners, was a freeze on real wages from 1970 to today. Now two wage earners are required for raising families. Exacerbating this disparity is that now over 50% of households are single parent households, so are under a major strain to provide. Wages for people at higher skill and educational levels have done much better.

> The impact on jobs that pay living wages has been unmerciful. Full employment doesn't mean those employed can afford to live or raise a family. In my research, and that of other groups, it takes a family of two, an income of at least $12.00 an hour each ($24.00 total) to afford the basics, and in many cities it is twice that much. Making the problem worse is that over half of households have single parent incomes.

Why are wages frozen? Companies balk at any outside pressure to raise wages. Investors keep intense pressure on companies to raise their profits every quarter so that stock prices go up. To do this, companies abandon research into technology that would produce innovation in production. So they have to buy other companies to get it. They don't do any employee training and expect employees to come to them fully trained.

> To maintain and increase profits is not some secret recipe. Companies have two general choices. 1) Increase revenue by selling more or raising prices. 2) Decrease production costs by reducing labor costs, or using cheaper materials. Reducing labor is the common option.

Middle size companies, including small businesses, make up around 90% of companies, and are better at creating jobs than corporations. But their competition is so intense many barely make a profit. They prefer to keep existing markets rather than expand. They hire more people than corporations and are responsible for around half of the nation's workforce numbers.

> Tech startups are the true technology innovators and create most of the new small business jobs.

Some have subscribed to the theory that reducing taxes and other ways of sending more money to business and investors would cause business to hire more people and raise wages. I personally have never seen a business I've managed in, from the largest to startups, ever mandate hiring more people. It just doesn't happen. During the last tax cut, companies didn't raise wages, add jobs, or bring back jobs from other countries, but instead bought back and split stock, creating higher stock prices for investors, with no impact on the worker or the economy.

Enriching business to create more jobs and higher wages is known as Supply Side Economics, or Trickle Down Economics, or Voodoo Economics. That theory has been fully disproved.

> Most of the income growth went to the top 1 percent and especially the top one-tenth of one percent of the population, who spend almost nothing back into the economy, but instead save or reinvest it. The US is now suffering from the highest level of income inequality of any time since the 1920s.[xxviii]

Will business change?

On the one hand, in the current environment, business is likely to continue doing the things that it has been forced to do that help it, but are overall destructive to workers and wages. They have no reason to change, but do have intense pressure from investors to continue doing these things. Major investors sit on the Boards of Directors, which makes governing decisions, and CEOs have stock included in their compensation packages, so there is major leadership incentive to please investors.

The only real hope is that as the labor market tightens, companies will pay higher wages to get good employees, rather than reverting to technology to radically eliminate jobs.

On the other hand, some CEOs and business schools have seen the danger signs and are promoting or adopting pro-social responsibilities.

Harvard Kennedy School for Business and Government, has its Social Responsibility Initiative[xxix]. It's premised partly on the idea of business sustainability[xxx]. "Several investors today use Environmental, Social, and Governance (ESG) metrics to analyze an organization's ethical impact and sustainability practices. Investors look at factors such as a company's carbon footprint, water usage, community development efforts, and board diversity." This should be on our wish list.

MIT and its Sloan School of Management is promoting the idea of a Social Contract in which employees, companies, and government all recognize responsibilities to each other. I've explored this idea myself for years, and it's a really good idea in theory. But in the current political and business economic climate, I don't see compelling reasons why companies or politicians would do it. Politicians and business organizations like the Chamber of Commerce would more likely sabotage it, as they have been doing. Social Contract should be on our wish list.

The Business Roundtable is a group of nearly 200 major US CEOs who are influential in government legislation. They recently put out a statement[xxxi] rejecting the primacy of stockholder interest in corporations, and instead noting the essential role of customers, employees, suppliers, and communities. Their statement wasn't without criticism from those who find it difficult to believe[xxxii]. This major change in attitude should also be on our wish list.

Investors are also looking at their role in sustainability, including their role in income inequality[xxxiii],[xxxiv].

How do we address the job and wage problem?

We have to address this systemic problem at a system level, which seems to be beyond our political leaders to see or acknowledge. Business leaders are looking at this, but a stock market correction, and Covid-19 pandemic, driving recession, as economists expect in 2020-2021, will cause leaders to contract on spending again.

We could organize as citizen unions that demand living wages and jobs. Or we could address it at a local level in which companies are tied to communities (important: not run by communities, which is Socialism).

Good and enduring success has been attained in many communities through a consortium of local business, local educator, philanthropic organizations and local government. This seems to be a recipe for success.

> **The primary way we need to address this** is to make sure people get the education they need to stay employed in jobs that pay well. This is key to making our people and communities thrive, rather than seeing them slowly fade into poverty and ruin. **This means lifetime education at work, community, trade school, and college, the subject of the chapter, *Preparing For The Future Of Education.***

Additional information is in the Chapter, *Toward a More Prosperous Economy For Everyone.*

Chapter 3: Preparing for the Future of Education

Colleges are not teaching what students require for the new jobs, and alternate education may be more qualifying for around 30% of jobs. Schools too often teach to pass tests on content knowledge. Other skills are needed. Delivery methods need to change so that as ever-changing work requires more post-secondary education, people can get it.

Over 90% of the jobs created since the Great Recession have required education beyond high school. But it may not be college. Georgetown University's Center on Education and the Workforce predicted that by 2020, 65% of the 55 million job openings would require some post-high school education.[xxxv]

The changing pattern of work required education:

- According to Brookings, the share of jobs requiring high and median digital skills between 2000 and 2016, went from 5% to 23%.

- Employment requiring medium skills went from 40% to 48%--almost half now.

- Employment requiring low skills went down dramatically, 56% to 30%.

In coming years:

- 30% of people will likely need a full college education

- 30% of people will need post-secondary education, such as trade schools.

- 30% will need a high school education or less.

The right education is essential to making a living that supports families. In most more rural areas, a two person household requires two people making a minimum of $12.00 an hour each to support independent living, and in large cities it is easily twice that much. (See Appendix 1.)

Over much of the last four decades, young college graduates have experienced lackluster wage growth. Wages for the bottom 50% of college graduates are lower today than they were in 2000.[xxxvi] But the upper 50% of wage earners in the US are mostly those with college degrees, other education, or who are just lucky to have good jobs.

While 34 percent of Americans ages 25 and older have a bachelor's degree or higher, only 26 percent of jobs currently require one.[xxxvii] Despite the fact that currently fewer than one-fifth of adults ages 21–24, have a college degree, "As of March (2019), the underemployment rate for workers aged 22 to 27 stands at 41.3%, according to the Federal Reserve Bank of New York." Part of the reason is because so many people have college degrees, so competition is very intense.

The reasons for this aren't straightforward. People with degrees are often overqualified because thirty percent of jobs don't require degrees but other education more relevant to the job. (26% of jobs don't require a Bachelors Degree.) Another reason is because people get lower jobs in companies just to have opportunity to move up. Another reason is that single people are waiting until average age 27 to marry and move out of their parent's homes. They use the time for career building, education, and who knows what.

The unemployment rate among young college graduates has fallen to pre-recession levels, but it is still higher than the full-employment economy of 2000. For young college graduates, the unemployment rate is 5.3 percent, compared with 5.4 percent in 2007 and 4.3 percent in 2000.

The overall employment rate for young college graduates has declined and the share who are idled has increased between 1990 and 2018.[xxxviii]

It's important to get it right, or sign up for a lifetime of low wages. Forty-three percent of those underemployed in first job out of college, in jobs not requiring a college degree, and are likely to stay that way through their career.) two-thirds are still underemployed after five years, and just over half remain so after ten years.[xxxix] And the problems is worse than in early 2000.[xl]

The demand will be highest for students with post-secondary education.

Demand will remain for some fields. According to federal estimates, four of the five occupational categories projected to add the most jobs to the economy over the next five years are among the lowest-paying jobs: "food preparation and serving" ($19,130 in average annual earnings), "personal care and service" ($21,260), "sales and related" ($25,360), and "health-care support" ($26,440). The difficulty for employers is that in many areas they can't find people for these jobs.[xli]

Teaching to a content test versus teaching workplace skills

It's often been said that physicians learn everything in medical school except a bedside manor. In most workplaces the ability to work with others and to have the skills to be an effective contributor, don't coincide with our competitive mindset.

Workers who can't work as a team with others, often prevent team success. They are often the first to be fired. Similarly those who can't adapt to a changing workplace or job requirements also find themselves without a job. The ability to work with a team, work across networks, communicate effectively, and use critical investigation and thinking, are critical to business. Tony Wagner's research (Senior Research Fellow and the Learning Institute, Harvard Innovation Lab)indicates that every young person will require a cores set of skills, which he expresses very well in this TEDx talk; https://www.youtube.com/watch?v=hvDjh4l-VHo.[xlii]

Requirements for new job types

New types of jobs aren't your old jobs. Collaboration, partnerships, agility and design thinking, creativity, problem-solving, and people skills will be needed. Unfortunately these aren't skills taught in the school system.

Kochan and Dyer[xliii] found that future competencies needed for work of the future tend to fall in three major categories.

"**One is technical skills**, or the **knowledge and capabilities that are specific to occupations or jobs**. Increasingly, particularly in companies that gravitate toward the augmentation approach to automation, these competencies will relate to what generally are described as information technology skills such as graphic design, coding, simulation modeling, and data analysis."

"**A second set** of competencies relates to **learning and innovation—or behavioral—skills such as creativity, critical thinking, teamwork, problem solving, communication, collaboration, negotiating skills, and the like.** These are particularly important for those who find themselves in or wanting to join companies that choose to implement high-road workplace practices."

"**The third set** of competencies has to do with **so-called life and career skills—socio-emotional attributes such as initiative and self-direction, flexibility and adaptability, personal responsibility, accountability, and agility—that help workers navigate in complex and rapidly changing work environments**."

Kochan and Dyer made their book *Shaping the Future of Work: A Handbook for Action and a New Social Contract* (MITxPress, 2017), available at a very low price in ebook form.

Various writers site the relevance of such skills as creativity, art, music, and interpersonal skills being necessary to a person's long-term adaptability and sustainability. In the book *Our Towns*, many recovering cities link arts to technological success. These things have been systematically drummed out of schools systems because of the focus on the Three Rs, teaching to the test, tight schedules, sports emphasis and budget constraints.

A number of skills are outlined that will be needed by future workers, that need to be taught in schools, is in this report. *Future skills, update and literature review,* prepared for Act Foundation, and the Joyce Foundation by Devin Fidler. *Institute for the Future.*[xliv]

People skills are a major part of it. You are likely to be asked to work with associates, and across cultures. You may be need to do this virtually. And you will likely need social intelligence to do this.

You will need not just the skills to work in your field, but also the ability to apply your knowledge and make sense of it. To be able to think in novel ways and adapt your thinking.

Additionally you will need workplace skills that include not just the ability to be there, but the ability to solve problems and make decisions. And instead of seeing all of your field material in one format, you will need the ability to understand material in other fields and forms, and to be cross-disciplinary in tour approach.

These skills fit well with Generation Z, who want the independence to seek out and solve challenges.

For more, Professor Emeritus Lee Dyer of Cornell University listed these skills this way:

- Ability to make sense of mass data. Critical thinkers.

- Ability to understand computer programming and modeling. Probably managers overview and experience. Ability to frame questions as problems, and analyzle solutions.

- Ability to use new media as tools. Remote workers share data with others.

- Ability to rank and tag content so not overwhelmed with mass and keep eye on important.

- Ability to collaborate with others in personal way. Assess feelings and adapt our presentation.

- Ability to lead remote teammates. Camaraderie and social presence.

- Ability to be agile. Comfortable with change. Novel and adaptive thinking. Aware of what is going on in the world to anticipate coming challenges. Be on leading edge of developing solutions in real time.

- Ability to understand the work environment so understand when change is necessary, and ability to create change solutions.

- Ability to be transdisciplinary – very strong in one discipline but knowledgeable and comfortable with other disciplines. Always learning.

These skills are very well explained in a PDF from Institute of the Future:
https://www.iftf.org/fileadmin/user_upload/downloads/wfi/ACTF_IFTF_FutureSkills-report.pdf

Testing

Many hate tests. Teaching to the test has also become hated. But are tests useful?

John Gabrieli, Investigator, McGovern Institute, and Director MIT Integrated Learning Initiative, "... science has shown ... that taking a test is one of the best ways of learning about the material in the long run. So if you could study something twice, and then you'll do better than if you study it once.

But if you study it once and then take a practice test on it, even when you give wrong answers and you're not corrected, your final performance is the best of all. So a practice test is better than spending more time studying something."

In my own experience in designing courses and presenting them, I use a number of techniques related to this. For example, I use questions about the material for timed reinforcement (from psychology of learning) at ever increasing intervals. I use quizzes that aren't for grades, that often reach back to earlier material. I engage students

with experiential problems that they solve. Post tests
indicate this works well even with those with learning
impediments like language.

Chapter 4: Education Delivery Methods

Following is a summary of important points about delivery methods, followed by how some aspects of alternative education can be accomplished.

Educational change drivers

- Colleges have priced themselves out of consideration by many

- Community colleges are offering more bachelor's degrees, generally with courses at 10% the cost of major colleges

- Business are needing more specific education for employees

- Technical school training is becoming more necessary

- Education closer to home, on a continuing basis, is needed as technology changes things

- Online education works, at a fraction of the cost

Online education is one way people can learn from home. It was developed through correspondence courses last century, then in the online digital age online degree schools like University of Pheonix and Edx. The Covid-19 pandemic drove all students from preschool to college to take their courses at home. Some colleges which curtailed classes for Spring 2020, also elected to present them online in the Fall of 2020.

Teachers who had to quickly change formats from classroom to online found that, even if they had experience with online teaching, it works but they needed more time to reconfigure material for online.[xlv]

Anecdotally, some students are finding they prefer online learning for several reasons. Learning is easier, they don't have to deal with difficult students, and they may prefer the conveniences of home.

Additionally a better selection of classes may be available to them and they can learn more at their own speed.

Finding ways to achieve success in online learning is essential. Since there may be minimal online interaction between students, part of the college experience can be missing, so dialogue with other students is essential. The online infrastructure is there to take advantage of with programs like Zoom which allow students to interact with each other visually.

Three types of models for online assisted learning

Colleges quickly continued the model of using TAs to do discussion groups with small groups of students. This continued the interactive dialogue, making the material much more engaging, which leads to success. But online courses in general have not gone to this model. They use discussion boards to enable students to comment. But these are not live or lively discussions. They are minimally engaging.

Model 1: The typical college model of small groups with a TA moderator, but doing it over Zoom, would allow students to communicate in real time, face to face, from all over the world. the discussion board would work for some, but others would benefit from dedicated hours and face to face.

Model 2: As delineated robustly in the next section of Part 2, groups of students could meet together in a physical space, get their lecture online, and discuss with each other and a qualified professor or industry professional with a teaching certificate. In this model, classes could be tailored to industry needs for local use, and standard classes could be taught without the need for driving to a college. This would make classes very accessible and continuing.

Model 3: The basic elements of Model 2 could be used to work in conjunction with local high schools to bring college education to the areas they serve. They are already doing this to some extent through dual credit courses that serve for both high school and college credit.

Model 3 would not grant degrees, which is State controlled, or be State supported, but certificates useful for employment. It would also provide a place for students to learn a variety of courses and obtain credit through CLEP Tests. It could also serve as a place for those taking online courses, or degree courses, to meet.

Online courses have abysmal completion rates. By providing the structure of meeting time, with a place to meet and discuss with other students and knowledgeable professors, it should make the completion rates much higher.

The Need for local, quality, higher education that leads to good jobs

Framing this issue, higher education in the community is a key to community economic development through availability of educated and trained human resources[xlvi]. This attracts and keeps businesses. It's a key to employment and better incomes for individuals and the community. It's a helpful key to career selection, which college students often don't decide until their Junior year.[xlvii]

Local education is very helpful in reducing the costs of a college education, by around $2000.00 each course ($594.00 credit hour).[xlviii] Costs continue increasing much faster than inflation,[xlix] and commonly take 10 to 25 years to repay.[l] Local classes make college courses accessible to students and the public.

A significant aspect of college spending is that completion rates tend to fall when government spending on education falls, and when open universities spread money too far.[li] This initiative will eliminate government spending, except grants, and increase meaningful completion rates in an open college with high academic standards. *Meaningful completion rates* means course completion after a trial class or period since this is not a degree offering. *Open* means no entrance requirements and access at very low cost.

Relevant to education is that the future is set for an economic battle featuring slow growth and many employment pressures.[lii,liii,liv] Despite current high employment, we have to prepare for a larger problem. Over the next 15+ years, around 30% of jobs will be replaced, displaced, or enhanced by Artificial Intelligence (AI) and Robotics, according to a McKinsey Institute continuing, deep study.[lv] "While we believe there will be enough work to go around (barring extreme scenarios), society will need to grapple with significant workforce transitions and dislocation. Workers will need to acquire new skills and adapt to the increasingly capable machines alongside them in the workplace. They may have to move from declining occupations to growing and, in some cases, new occupations."[lvi] This means education.

Competition and investors will require these educational changes, such as we are seeing in McDonalds and Walmart. Investors require companies to earn at quarterly guidance expectations or they dump shares, destroying iconic companies like Sears (retail is always hazardous) and GE, which was unthinkable, but both became noncompetitive. With a lackluster economy and unrelenting pressure from investors to boost stock prices, companies will struggle to achieve cheaper operations, which means foregoing research and expansion, price increases, and job replacement by technology.[lvii]

Many fields are ripe for employee replacement. Robotics and AI work especially well in structured environments, such as repeat mechanical processes and structured data. Common jobs. AI is improving rapidly with unstructured data as well, as demonstrated by Google and IBM supercomputers.

Job replacement includes such fields as certain lawyers and physicians. For example, cell counting, biological testing, and some of cancer diagnostics is done by computer, and done more accurately than by techs or physicians. But as an enhancement to doctors, it becomes even more accurate. AI impacts especially hard those jobs that don't require human decision making, such as counting cells, retail and manufacturing. Around 50% of jobs can be automated, displacing 6 of 10 workers.[lviii] There is no 1:1 replacement of workers, but knowledge in certain areas will be critical for developing, implementing, and maintaining these technologies and what they advise or control.

Especially vulnerable is the low end of the financial scale, which can become a burden on community resources. With fourteen percent of the US population in Poverty status, the largest vulnerable distribution is female age 25-34, followed by female 35-44.[lix] This becomes very significant considering that these are child raising years and over 50% of US households are now headed by a single parent. Insufficient household income puts children in poverty as well. Fast food and retail, which are common jobs in this income category, will be severely impacted and people will need more education to get better jobs. They can get it only if it is available.

Aggregate demand for many products has likely peaked in the US and Europe.[lx] Previous major changes in the US job market have been driven by the industrial and technology revolutions, agricultural shifts to city jobs, rapid population growth, WWII technology transfers, rapid technology innovation for new products, and 3 to 4% inflation. These are minimal economic drivers in today's world. Population growth is nearly stabilized just as Europe did several decades ago, many technology driven fields have peaked with few innovations coming (except medical, AI, and Robotics), military operations have minor impact on today's technology, and annual inflation and GDP are both likely to remain at 2 to 2.5%. (Electronics may gain new components, but not revolutionize the world.)

Lower incomes are affecting new generations and demand. Millennials have indicated they aren't as much into consumerism, rather experiences and quality, and they don't have money to waste.[lxi] Discretionary personal income drives the economy,[lxii, lxiii] and on average it goes up with income increases. But raises are going disproportionately to the upper half of the economic classes, who save instead of spending. Personal credit card debt is rising,[lxiv] depleting disposable income. These things impact spending, so consumer demand is stable to only slowly rising.[lxv]

Economic expansion and jobs will be buffeted by these headwinds. If not addressed well, these changes will have severe impact on employment, personal incomes, community economics, and taxes.

Largely, these job replacements must be addressed by education, and this is what brings community and individual prosperity and well being.

Many State Legislatures have approved more cooperation between high schools, community colleges, and public four year colleges, to streamline educational trajectories and focus on courses that transfer credit. Colleges in the past have been rejecting 45% of credit transfers. Four year colleges are fighting to keep their place in the system. Core courses are being identified. See Addendums 1, 2, and 3.

Communities have to take measures to protect themselves. College education becomes ever more necessary for knowledge and skills, but colleges continue to push costs to unaffordable levels, and states and communities can't take on the additional burdens of funding colleges.[lxvi] So this is the time to take the initiative and solve this problem.

This proposal is minimally theoretical and mostly practical. It shows what is realistically possible with support using conservative estimates, showing student education costs can be lowered to under 10% of regular college courses, while maintaining high quality and making it much more accessible and attainable. Higher education can and should be brought to communities.

Some states are leading the way with credential pathways that lead to jobs that pay livable wages. They are partnering with resources such as the National Skills Coalition and Education Strategy Group, (https://m.nationalskillscoalition.org/resources/publications/file/9.1

8-NSC_QNDC-paper_web.pdf and
http://edstrategy.org/resource/building-credential-currency/) to
guide them.

Some institutions have partnered with MIT and other colleges in
special programs.[lxvii]

The well supported *Every Learner Everywhere* organization offers
resources for online educators to improve course design, teaching,
and learning in online environments.[lxviii]

 "Developed by the Online Learning Consortium, the Association
of Public and Land-grant Universities, and Every Learner
Everywhere, with support from the Bill & Melinda Gates
Foundation, the playbook provides a path for continuous
improvement of instruction along a quality-oriented continuum.[lxix]

• Design guides immediate and basic needs for moving a course
online. It is useful for translation of face-to-face or blended courses
for fully-online delivery.

• Enhance provides options to strengthen the student learning
experience. It is useful for improving face-to-face course elements
that do not translate easily to online modalities.

• Optimize offers ideas and resources for online teaching that
aligns with high-quality, evidence-based instructional practices. It
is useful for continuous improvement of the online learning
experience and student outcomes."

Chapter 5: Developing a quality Community higher education program

Post-secondary education doesn't have to be expensive. Ventures in education tend to think in terms of permanent classrooms and faculty facilities, large permanent staffs, state sanctioned degrees, and financing through community taxes and tuition. This puts post-secondary education out of consideration for many communities, which means that people who need it will never have access to it. Individuals and communities suffer.

If history in the last and this century has taught us anything, things change rapidly and business and education have to be nimble and adaptable to keep up. We can also look around and see that many people could have better jobs or pursue their dreams if they could just get access to education.

The purpose of this chapter is not to create an alternate system of education, but to show how by thinking outside of the box, communities can use rented facilities, available temporary professors and subject matter experts, online resources, business leaders, outside educational and business advisors, CLEP tests, online diplomas, and dual credit high school courses, at very affordable rates, to offer community citizens viable educational pathways to better jobs and careers, which are **very significant goal endpoints**.

A major benefit of online delivery to local classes is the ability of students to talk with each other about the subject matter. Discussion is a great benefit to learning, and would help completion rates for courses.

A secondary benefit is that community continuing education courses could be offered in the same building spaces, defraying the cost of space rental. It may also help school systems and local facilities like churches and shopping centers, with expenses through renting their spaces.

Another major need is remedial classes. Around a third of college students need remedial classes.

A final benefit is that doing things without government sponsorship avoids the tax burden and government control. Community cooperatives for many services are becoming more and more popular. They substantially lower the cost and keep the service under community control.[lxx]

Experiential education

While educational streamlining is the goal of the government, young adults often need more extensive experiential exposure in subjects before college majors are selected. We can rob students of this opportunity in traditional education, which is a huge waste of time and resources. Many students leave college dissatisfied with their career field selections, which are required choices by their third year. Course emphasis should be on courses that explore careers, especially through projects, so that students make informed choices of careers.

Cost and accessibility

Classes should be open to all students (no entry qualifications), and at very affordable rates (1/10th college rates).

Structurally such an effort would likely be a nonprofit, private, collaborative educational organization. Community led efforts in many things are becoming very popular and giving control to the local people. High schools generally have government approval to offer dual H.S-college credit courses. For many courses there will be transfer credit for approved core courses. There will be a small cost to students for courses and no tax base support. It potentially could be supported by grants from interested parties and those organizations that benefit from the college. But it could be simply tuition supported, with assistance to those who need it.

Targeted educational goals for relevant courses and sources

The primary target educational goals should be preparation for new jobs displaced by AI and robotics, which are most important to community and business well being. These are mostly service jobs, including healthcare providers, professionals such as engineers, scientists, accountants, and analysts; IT professionals and other technology specialists; managers and executives, whose work cannot easily be replaced by machines; educators, especially in emerging economies with young populations.

Additionally in increasing demand will be, "creatives," a small but growing category of artists, performers, and entertainers who will be in demand as rising incomes create more demand for leisure and recreation; builders and related professions, particularly in the scenario that involves higher investments in infrastructure and buildings; manual and service jobs in unpredictable environments, such as home-health aides and gardeners.[lxxi]

Development of this higher education service will happen in the phases outlined below, with the assistance of a task force.

Sources

High quality educational online courses are available at zero to very low cost, such as from MIT and Harvard.[lxxii] MIT is a premier technical college with a heavy commitment to sharing its courses in a robust way, with zero to minimal cost. Most major colleges offer these Massive open online course (MOOCS) through Edx.org, Teachable.com, Coursera.org, Udacity.com, and many other providers. Many degrees are available from these colleges through these platforms, even including 45 Masters Degrees from universities around the world. MOOCS degrees are substantially lower in price than standard online degree programs. And they are self-paced.

A task force would need to refine the following figures more thoroughly, determine local needs, and determine organizational structure.

General Educational Focus

- Student and graduate career educational experience
- Student and graduate college level education
- Manufacturing and service business needs
- City and County administrative, operation, and police needs
- General community education needs

Specific Goals

Enable students and others to:

- Experience college or trade school course work and get transferable credit, and gain confidence through top educational material
- Enable students and others to experience new careers through subject matter material
- Get a head start on technical school or college for certificates, 2 year, or 4 year
- Obtain college level transferable credits at affordable prices
- Prepare and qualify for local or other work and promotions, to enhance the work force
- Get Continuing Education courses and credits (Credit or non-credit)
- Get education without travel, at very affordable rates.

For the community:

- Assist local businesses and government with qualified personnel, and in education and training.
- Provide employment opportunities in education.
- Provide opportunities for Community Education, scholastic or non-scholastic efforts.
- Each student have a specific goal to reach.

Initiatives to develop a community educational organization would probably best be done in phases so that corrections can be made without adversely affecting the end goal.

Development Phases

Phase 1, first year, Endorsements and Planning: Gain endorsements of local government leaders, teachers, companies, schools, and students, to indicate both need and approval. Review education resources; survey of student, business, and community needs; planning of courses; potential attendance; potential professors and instructors; location of potential classrooms with no campus, pay scales, costs, revenue, administrative needs and personnel.

Phase 2, Proof of Concept: Establish 5 Fall and 10 Spring classes from surveyed needs and interests. Evaluate and move to Phase 2 if successful.

Phase 3, Resources: Resource gathering and potential commitments. Student recruiting. Implementation.

Phase 4 Evaluation and planning: Evaluation of Phase 1 - 3 results. Planning for additional courses.

Phase 5, Evaluation of results and future needs. Evaluate the need for a campus. Possible community bond issuance for financing.

Risk Management

A venture would come with a lot of variables, making it difficult to predict. To avoid financial risk, studies will be completed early by qualified volunteers to verify the veracity of this approach to education in your area, outline any problems that can be foreseen and ways to overcome, and to determine success factors that should be implemented.

A steering committee, or board of directors, should be organized, and specific goals set. At this point, members of the board should get an honorarium payment to acknowledge the value of their volunteer work and displacement of other things they could be doing to earn income. Consider $10,000.00 for a year commitment.

Teachers should be paid primarily from collected course fees. Grants could also help.

The first fall and spring offerings should indicate if this can move ahead without significant risk.

Specific risks

1. Insufficient attendance to pay for professors.
2. Insufficient attendance to pay classroom lease commitments.
3. Inability to find and retain enough professors or subject matter experts with teaching certificates.
4. The lack of institution accreditation may impact willingness of professors to teach.
5. Dropouts (30%) can require fees back, causing disturbance.
6. Teacher leaves without backup.
7. High student failure rate.
8. Insurance (an expense, not a risk).
9. Lack of area knowledge about emergency services.

10.	Sexual and other harassment

11.	Lack of counseling

12.	Other colleges oppose this type of education

Risk control

- Insufficient attendance: Withdraw course if insufficient attendance. Write into teacher contracts.

- Lease: Use flexible property that is free or can use rent instead of lease (school, churches, open retail spaces).

- Lack of accreditation: Online courses and degrees are from accredited institutions.

- Student drops, wants fee: No dropout fee return after the first two weeks of classes.

- Professor leaves: Have a list of teachers, and less qualified, who can step in if a teacher leaves, since the primary course delivery is online.

- High failure rate: Change to pass-fail option for failing students, or no credit.

- Insurance: Use school system for insurance.

- Emergency services: Make sure all teachers and classrooms have emergency procedures and numbers circulated and posted.

- Professors unable to design courses. Get them help or get someone else to design the course. (Edx has courses on this)

- Sexual and other harassment: Make sure all students are informed. Show a film and distribute pamphlets on the first class. Establish independent reporting.

- Counseling: Career counseling is not an option at this point. Maybe Later.

- College opposition: Address the high quality and low cost
  with students. Colleges are more likely to oppose
  accreditation, with the State.

Professors and Teachers

Many identified courses could be taken online without a professor present, but would be more effective in a classroom setting due to class discussion, ability to ask questions from professors, and increased commitment. Failure to complete online courses is a notable problem with online courses. For example Missouri WGU has a four year completion rate of 20 to 49% compared with a 70% rate for attended colleges.[lxxiii] (They all like to fudge statistics.)

Most of the courses listed later can be accompanied by just an instructor, but for maximum benefit a qualified professor should be present. Courses can also be taken online with no instructor, and missed classes can be attended online. The course format removes some of the class preparation and expertise level from professors.

Generally credit during Phase 1-3 would be achieved through CLEP tests or tests administered by the course sponsoring organization, so course accreditation isn't an issue and credits would be transferable.

The professor, through education or experience, should be able to answer questions or find answers. If necessary, he should be able to integrate course material to achieve the knowledge necessary for the CLEP test. Many of these courses are primarily delivered by video with electronic text books or reading. Eventually course development will lead to this institution's own accredited courses.

Qualified professors for various types of classes:

- Masters Degree or Doctorate.

- College Teachers Assistant (TA) working on masters or doctorate

- High school teacher with Masters Degree

- High school teacher with Bachelors Degree

- Trade school instructor

- Local business or industry professional with subject matter proficiency

Supply of professors

- Fifty-nine percent of H.S. teachers have a post-graduate degree, with usually many close high schools. Many areas have retired teachers who would like to continue teaching a less burdensome schedule. These are likely within close driving range for evenings and weekends.

- There are generally many colleges and technical colleges within close driving range.

- There are usually many business professionals in the area who can provide professional input to courses.

Class schedule

Monday - two hour class length on two week days, or 3 hour intensives

Saturday - two hour class length on two days, or 3 hour intensives

Evening – One to two hour class length on 2 to 3 evenings

Monday and Saturday intensives (3 hour sessions)

Summer – daily, evening, and weekend classes

Other as determined.

Chapter 6: Course Purposes

The courses should be a mix that tries to give students:

- A taste of a career through basic knowledge (intro courses, especially with labs and hands on)

- Remedial, and those essential H.S courses needed for college entrance, accelerated

- Courses that give students a head start in college

- Courses that can eliminate up to the first two years of a four year college.

- Courses needed for local businesses and government.

- Sequential course access over two semesters and summer intensive, and two years.

Course Material Quality

The source of course material is essential to course quality, effectiveness, and satisfaction. Courses must be eligible for transfer credit through the course exam or CLEP. Course grades may be important for college admittance.

Colleges don't accept GPAs from other colleges. They just accept course or CLEP credits. Most four year colleges want students to spend the last year or two at their college for the student to be eligible for a degree. CLEP credits are typically limited to 100 and 200 level courses. MITx (through Edx) offers tests for higher level courses. Coursera offers degrees. Also available are online Bachelors and Masters Degrees from major universities for 42% of the on campus cost.

Sources

MIT, technology focused, provides free "Open University" undergrad and graduate courses, online text books, video, and exams.[lxxiv] They provide no certificate or degree, so CLEP tests would be used for transfer credit. Some courses are specifically for AP testing.

"CLEP exams cover intro-level college course material in 33 subjects. A passing score on just one CLEP exam can save you 100+ hours of class time and coursework and up to $1,200 [$2200] in tuition."

MIT courses can be mixed with other courses and delivered by a professor.

You can also use MITx free online courses which offer a certificate for ~$100.00 for business use.[lxxv] Certificates are not college credit, and can't transfer, but are useful to business needs. Free OpenCourseWare is also available from Yale, Harvard, Stanford, UC Berkeley, Carnegie Mellon, and many other universities.[lxxvi]

MIT courses offer excellent education, instructor insights, video lectures, lecture notes, free electronic text books, and guest lectures, lab guides, and instructor training, all free.

Coursera, offers many courses, which are $49.00 per month for continuous enrollment and no course fee. Courses culminate in certificates, college credit, and degrees, up to Masters. Courses feature interactive textbooks, prerecorded videos, quizzes, and projects. They feature the world's best education sources, partnering with top universities and organizations. Over 1,700 companies use Coursera to train their employees. Coursera courses are usually ACE accredited, but not all.

Udemy, similar to Coursera. Courses start at $13.00 each. Generally offers certificates.

An example of possible courses from a preliminary selection of 45 mostly MIT student courses

Courses for teachers

OCW Educator Portal for teachers (not part of the 45 student courses)
To teach an MIT course, teachers should take this course of these brief lectures.

There are also notes on teaching each available class.

Explore Instructor Insights to discover how MIT instructors teach with these materials on campus, and freely select and adapt their explanations, examples, and simulations to help concepts come to life in your own classroom. (Courses can be redesigned for CLEP test material)

Creating a space for students to discover their passion for chemistry

5.111SC Principles of Chemical Science.

Video course on teaching college level science and engineering – graduate level

Lecture 1: General Principles of Teaching (video)

Lecture 2: Teaching Equations

Lecture 3: Taking Account of Misconceptions; Avoiding Rote Learning

Lecture 4: Designing Homework and Exam Problems

Lecture 5: Course Design

Class Session 3: Designing a Course: Developing Learning Outcomes

Class Session 5: Teaching Methodologies, Part II: Active Learning: Why and How

Lecture 6: Teaching Interactively in Large and Small Groups

Lecture 7: Lecture Planning and Performing

Lecture 8: Teaching with Blackboards and Slides

Lecture 9: Political Barriers to Educational Change

Lecture 10: Course Summary and Your Questions

45 Student Courses

Anthropology (MIT)

Intro to Anthropology
How Culture Works
Identity and Difference

Forensics

Intro to Forensic Science – Coursera

Forensic Accounting and Fraud Examination – Coursera

Digital Computer Forensics – Udemy

Other Forensic Science courses

Electrical Engineering and Computer Science (MIT)

Programming

Information technology

Signal Processing Prereq Calculus. (Laplace Transforms and Fourier Series)

Remedial math, English, and other courses

Aerodynamics

Aeronautical knowledge for flying (MIT)

Aerodynamics

Introduction to Aerospace Engineering and Design (MIT. Significant material costs. Prereq: freshman level physics, mathematics, and chemistry. Team builds a lighter than air plane.)

Biological Sciences (MIT) Quantitative aspects of biology

Molecular biology

Biochemistry

Genetics

Cell biology

Biological Engineering (MIT)

Molecular, Cellular, and Tissue Biomechanics

Business

Managerial Accounting Fundamentals – Coursera

Accounting Analytics – Coursera

Business Analytics – Coursera

Marketing

Business law

Six Sigma Methods (MIT - related to productivity)

Leadership (MIT)

Project Management (MIT)

Negotiation, Mediation, and Conflict Resolution (Essec Business School through Coursera)

Graduate courses: Organizational Behavior (MIT)

Leading Teams (U of Michigan, through Coursera)

Understanding harassment, sexual and otherwise (Community Ed, no credit)

Conflict Resolution (UCI through Coursera, certificate only)

Four courses plus project.

Healthcare

History

Communications

Freshmen Composition

Public Relations

Intro to journalism

Economics (MIT)

Micro Economics

Macro Economics

Humanities (MIT)

Psychology

Sociology

Early childhood education

Literature (MIT)

Foundations of Western Culture

Foundations of World Culture

Mathematics (MIT)

Uncertainty In Engineering

Single Variable Calculus

Multi-variable Calculus

Math for Computer Science

Intro to Probability and Statistics

Mechanical Engineering (MIT)

Engineering Dynamics

Intro to Heat Transfer

Materials Science (MIT)

Thermodynamics of Materials

Political Science (MIT)

Political Philosophy – Global Justice

Feminist Thought

Philosophy of Law

American Political Thought

Citizenship and Pluralism

Teacher training (MIT)

Community Education – no credit - taught by local skilled or qualified personnel. Not included in the selected 45 courses.

Conflict Resolution

Dancing

Health for Seniors

Senior Living

Community business development

Public Relations

Building in Basements, meeting code

Marriage and Relationship Enhancement

Acting for stage and TV

Semester 2: creating a play

Writing for entertainment - Prereq: Acting for stage and TV

Family budgeting

Business Writing

Technical Writing

Energy storage and efficiency

Plastics recycling into new products

Chapter 7: Course costs

Based on 15 courses per semester, with accelerated 15 summer classes on year 2

Teaching staff costs, based on annualized professor salary of $70,000.00 per year.

Payment of $30 to 34.00 per hour, 3 credit classes, 45-48 contact hours, x 1.5 prep time = $2208.00 per course. A class of 10 students would pay a maximum of $220.00 for a course.

Based on 45 total courses per year, professor cost of all course offering = $99,360.00.

Lab material for 1/3 of classes = $300.00 ave. x 15 = $4,500.00

Class room materials: 15 projectors (for computers) at $200.00 ea. = $3000.00

Electronic text books – usually from MIT and other institutions – Free

Lease space at .70 per square foot per month.

½ of classes at a high school – no charge.

Rental of local church space, retail space, other space, 15x20 x .70 per sq.' x 12months x 15 rooms = $38,000.00

Administrative cost (part time) – ½ paid volunteer year 1:

Three board members, including president, x $10,000.00 = $30,000.00

Communications associate services = $5000.00

Tests (CLEP paid for by students at time of testing: $89.00 (Or MITx test at ~$100.00)

Total Costs*

Professors: $100,000.00

Lab material: $5,000.00

Lease Space; $38,000.00

Administrative Costs: $3,500.00

Classroom tech; $3000.00

Total Costs: $181,000.00

* Does not include community courses, which should work out the same.

Likely attendance—cost per student

350 potential students to serve based on 70% typical college enrollment

Conservative 50% take 2 courses per year (708 students).

Conservative 25% take 6 courses per year (531 students).

75%, (266) total enrollment. (1239 total students in courses)

Average student cost per class: $181,000/1239 students = $146.00 per course, plus $89.00 exam if necessary, 7% of a typical course at a college.

First course is free unless for credit.

$438.00 average cost per year, per student, for 3 courses each, or $146.00 each class.

(Recommend the cities, counties, and businesses pay up to ½ of tuition [grants] on a sliding scale. If the college gets accredited, Pell grants can also help cover tuition.)

Comparison to community college

Typical Community Colleges raise $350,000.00 a year through taxes, based on an average home value of $166,000.00, 12,000 households, $29.00 per household. This varies by geographical area. The tuition cost per student runs about the same.

This community education plan takes no money from taxes (households), and costs only 7% of typical college courses, with guaranteed excellent courses.

If the community education organization wanted to get facilities, get accredited, and offer degrees

Future accredited college cost with buildings on property

ACE college accreditation: Regional accreditation ensures that an institution's academic program meets or exceeds acceptable levels of quality and is the most recognized accreditation status for higher education entities.

Teacher accreditation is a mandatory requirement under the Teacher Accreditation Act 2004 that teachers are accredited at Proficient Teacher Level, and maintain that accreditation, with the National Education Standards Authority (NESA). ... Accreditation at Highly Accomplished and Lead level is voluntary.

39 year amortization period (if used)

1050 enrollment

45 concurrent classes

Land: (under) $675,000.00

13,500 sq' class building, 1000 sq.' administrative building, (no dorms or cafeteria) $100.00 sq.' construction cost = $1,350,000

Corporate bond for 20 years, 100 investors at $20,250.00 @ 5% interest, $500.00 annual coupon x 100 = $50,000.00

Overseer of maintenance, sanitation, grounds, and janitorial per year = $55,000.00

Janitor services at .05/sq.' per hour (mostly students-aid), 1 hr./day = $200,000.00

Utilities at .13 per sq.' = $1885.00 per mo., per year = 22,620.00

Building maintenance, starting at year 3, $12.00 per sq.' = $174,000.00

6 full time administrative personnel @ $75,000.00 = 450,000.00

Insurance = $1000.00 per month = $12,000.00

Total annual costs = with corporate bond coupon = $975,620.00

Cost per student = $929.00 a year

(Probably around $1000.00 per student per year, which is <10% of 4 year college costs)

Chapter 8: Toward a More Prosperous Economy For Everyone

People tend to look at the economy like a pie with only so many viable pieces available to serve from a it. It's kind of kitchen table economics.

This is an intuitive approach for most people. They have fixed budgets. They have a certain amount of money coming in, a certain amount going out, and if they're lucky they have a little left over for "discretionary spending." It's intuitive that the nation's economy works the same. But it doesn't.

This view of the economy leads to restrictions that prevent growth. I'll talk about growth mechanisms in a moment, but first understand the problem.

Most of us look at our wallets to decide whether our economy is healthy or not. Economists have a wide range of measures they can look at. But many people simply look at GDP, the national pie, because they compare one country with another and always want to be on top.

GDP is the overall value of national economic activity – the total national value of goods and services. GDP means diddly squat to most people. It's not a good reference to national wellbeing because it doesn't take into account how well individuals are faring in the economy. (GDP per capita [dollars per individual] is a better figure for that – the US ranks 19th in the world, $59,000.00 compared to the top performer $139,000.00.)

But that figure is also misleading in that the average is skewed by a large number of high earners at the top of the scale and a large number of low earners at the low end of the scale. Instead of seeing an even distribution across the economy, we see huge numbers at either end.

Imagine that the population is split in half, with high earners being in the top half, and low earners being in the low half. In reality this is the way it is, with average household income at $60,000.00. The upper half are doing well, and they contribute much to GDP, the pie. Low earners are not doing well, with many unable to earn a wage that allows them to live on their own and raise a family. They contribute very little to GDP, and get very little from the pie.

The intuitive response to difficult times is austerity. Austerity means you cut spending to match your income. It means that there is very little discretionary income to spend.

A major difficulty of reducing discretionary spending is that discretionary spending is a major driver of the economy. Business and GDP fall when there is less discretionary spending.

Essentially what we have in the US is half the nation living on low incomes, and around 40% of them depending on government assistance to even make ends meet. Deferred medical treatment costs our national safety net more in the long run. So what we have 40% of people being a drag on the economy, and 50% being weak contributors to GDP, the pie.

The pathetic thing is we tend to keep things this way. Our lack of vision fixes this economy in place. After reviewing the realities of Capitalism, we'll get back to the pie distribution theory.

False narratives on Capitalism

We live with a false narrative about our economic system. We're Capitalists. But Capitalism didn't grow on a tree. It's an invention by people. It is what we make it to be. We can make it work for all of us, and that's well within our Constitution. And that doesn't mean becoming Socialist, which has been proven from experience not to work very well.

We need to understand some things.

The idea promoted by many, is pure capitalism, Laissez Faire economics, which means "leave it lone," in the belief that market forces will work themselves out. It doesn't make any difference how many lives it destroys while it works. This is based on Adam Smith's economic treatise in the early 1700s.

Today we have cities with twenty million people in their metropolitan areas. When the market works itself out, we don't grow and can vegetables in our back fields, nor do we grow chickens in our back yard, nor do we hunt game in the forest. In most cities those things would get you thrown in jail. We depend on each other to buy our products and services that we're paid wages to provide.

We also don't have companies that operate by pure capitalism. The values of pure capitalism are that industries control the production and sale of goods, and then supply, demand, and competition are driving market forces. Except it doesn't really work that way. We can create economic Demand Curves all day long and it doesn't mean a thing.

Companies make forecasts to sell a certain amount to please investors. Then they control supply, and they have an impact on demand, plus they escape competition. Does that sound like pure capitalism?

Companies simply estimate the amount of product they think they will sell, use advertising to manipulate the market, and buy their competitors so they don't have any competition, so they can control prices. That doesn't mean that business is easy. It just means business has had centuries to perfect what they do. Pure capitalism and Laissez Faire economics are simply myths used to discourage interference in the markets from the public and politicians.

We need to improve our social systems so that people don't suffer in our system. But we definitely want to keep things about Capitalism that make it work well, and these things have been appropriated even by countries with Socialist Command economic systems like Cuba and China.

- Individual initiative is rewarded so that people want to create new things.

- Competition benefits consumers with new and better products.

- Individual choice of occupations

We can do whatever we want with our economic system to make it work for everyone. And we can make it work better. It just takes knowledge and political or citizen power.

Back to the pie

Imagine if wages were at the point that all wage earners were above the middle line. GDP would likely be at least 50% higher, not quite double what it is. The pie would be much larger. (This is an oversimplification, but it's not misleading.)

What would the effect be of moving wages to at least livable wages, and getting closer to everyone being above the middle line, say above $60,000.00 household income in 2020?

People who make higher wages have more discretionary income. They provide more revenue to small business and services. The US is primarily a service economy, and small business hires 80% of the nation's people. Small business would thrive despite paying larger wages to people.

Those at the top end would do well as well. The wealthy always do well because they get most of their income through stock, largely from increases in stock prices. All during the 2008 Great Recession years, major corporations and stock holders made record profits. The difficulty with them is that they don't spend their money back into the economy. They either invest in stock or remove their money from circulation. Removing money from circulation kills the economy.

By raising wages of the lower half, then welfare and Medicaid, and other government assistance would cease to be Federal and State budget spending items. While Medicare is solvent for the Federal Government for years into the future, Medicaid is a budget killer for States.

There is concern that raising wages will simply cause rising prices, driving an inflationary spiral like what developed in the 1970s. The Federal Reserve is responsible for controlling inflation. They generally do this by controlling Federal Reserve lending interest rates, and they have ceased to use inflation as a factor.

So the best place to invest in America and the wellbeing of others is to raise the wages of the lower half of the scale. Raising the minimum wage pushes other wages up. Everyone gets a boost. The economy gets a boost.

To make this happen we need good paying jobs for everyone. There are at least three ways to do this.

First, the government can hire people and give them jobs. Everyone hates this method. To pay workers, the government has to raise taxes. Unless we start printing money out of thin air, which is never what we actually do despite the myths, it's not a good method.

> It's true that you can't save or starve your way to prosperity. Taxes take away. It's possible that they may create new jobs, but it removes discretionary income from people, which deflates the economy.

Second, wage increases. As wages go up, company profit goes down, so stock prices go down, disappointing investors. Small businesses object to wage raises because it makes them noncompetitive. But it isn't as bad as it sounds. For example in areas where fast food restaurants raised minimum wages, none went out of business and it had a positive effect on the economy of the area.

> In reality, boosting wages from $7 to $12.00 an hour has a minimal effect on fast food prices. It raises the price of a hamburger 12 cents. Similarly in manufacturing, if a person creates 20 products in an hour, raising his wage $5.00 raises the price of the product by 25 cents. Stock holders also get

a boost in earnings. There is no inflation.

> In service industries where manpower is the primary factor, the effect raising wages has depends on the length of the work. A dollar an hour raise for a job that takes four hours, raises the price of the job by $4.00 plus benefits based on wages.

When wages are raised across the board, they stay competitive with other businesses, including in-house services they compete with inside other businesses. So the impact on raising wages in our 80% service economy, overall has less than a 1 to 1 wage to price ratio. It increases discretionary income which promotes the overall economy and makes everyone wealthier.

Companies become more profitable through wage increases. So objections to wages going up are hollow arguments. We need to understand company kickback as knee jerk reactions because companies thrive on the status quo and don't like interference.

Third, increase the number of jobs is through new businesses. US population and job shifts over the last 150 years have taught us many things about jobs and economics. Rather than destroy our economy, demand for new products creates more jobs. Farming used to be 90% of our economy. As technology and mechanization replaced farm jobs, ending back breaking labor that shortened lives, people moved to less rural areas and found jobs. This is still going on.

With more people in cities to sell to, with discretionary dollars to spend, new businesses evolved, bringing many new products. They hired more people. The mainstay jobs of the past, agriculture and manufacturing, today total only around 20% of the workforce.

More types of jobs develop with more money available for spending. How does this work? Large businesses, like corporations, are not job creators. In fact, they are net job destroyers. Smaller businesses have less growth. Entrepreneurs are actually the job creators today. They create new products. They hire people.

All of this sounds like we could just spur entrepreneurial job growth. And this would be a good thing to do. We have incubators all around the country that try to spur new product development for the betterment of communities (and enrichment of investors). We also have universities doing all kinds of research that lay the basis for new products. And this is an important feature of the new economy.

But we have to pause for a moment to consider what else is happening in our world, and how we can harness this.

Thirty percent job displacement through Artificial Intelligence and automation.

We are already past the tipping point on this happening, so it's not conjecture. It will continuing taking place over the next fifteen years. It's making the job earnings scene more difficult. Wages as a share of GDP have fallen by roughly 8 percent since 1970. Nearly all the benefits of economic growth have been captured by large corporations and their shareholders.

After-tax corporate profits have doubled from about 5 percent of GDP in 1970 to about 10 percent. And the wealthiest 1 percent's share of pre-tax income has more than doubled, from 9 percent in 1973 to 21 percent today. Taken together, these two trends amount to a shift of more than $2 trillion a year from the middle class to corporations and the super-rich.[lxxvii]

The 30% of jobs that don't currently require post-secondary education are unlikely to be affected. But those jobs usually don't pay well. They're in the bottom half of the wage distribution. The half that needs lifted up.

The jobs that will be hit hardest are those that can be automated by Artificial Intelligence (AI), and those are jobs that handle data but don't require human judgment. Loan application vetting is an example. A simple program can pull together qualifying facts from input and then pass it on to someone for a final evaluation.

In the medical field, computers look at scans for cancer cells. They are more accurate than doctors because they have the benefit of experience of thousands of scans that doctors have evaluated. But together with a doctor's assessment they are extremely accurate. So doctors' jobs get displaced, but in their new capacity they get assisted by AI. Radiology is not looking like a growth field. The same is happening in the legal field.

People who work in factories are likely to get displaced by robotics. Any physical process that doesn't require human judgment can be replaced by robotics, or displaced by it. One person can oversee multiple processes that used to be done by multiple people.

The impact of this is people are going to have to become better educated to work in the new environment. Over 90% of jobs created since the Great Recession have required education beyond high school. People who go to cities to find work, find they aren't prepared. And the new jobs require education that isn't being delivered by traditional sources like colleges. The Covid-19 rush to online education proves that we can do it.

To accommodate this need for education, it will have to be closer to individual's homes, be ongoing to keep up with the evolving workplace, and be financially available to everyone. It will have to include the new types of skills and knowledge required for the new jobs, and will also have to be tailored to regional and local needs. This means there will be a lot of new educational job opportunities.

On top of recession caused job-wage displacement, and Covid-19 caused unemployment, this provides another level of complication for jobs and the economy. Yet institutions like MIT (various professors) think that fewer will be displaced than replaced, and this will all work out with new types of jobs.

It will work out if we encourage education and new job creation.

Toward job and wage growth

The mechanisms that are needed to create a more robust economy for everyone are:

- Provide wages that support families. Over 50% of households now are led by single parents. Poverty level wages, and those with children working two jobs to support their family, are unconscionable. We certainly can do better in a very wealthy nation.

- Raise the minimum wage, which will raise everyone's wages without affecting competition. This will also benefit the economy. It will eliminate most people's need for government financial assistance, ending dependency programs. With higher wages people can afford more products at higher prices.

- Create new jobs through entrepreneurial companies and universities to increase the workforce to employ everyone. This can also be a financial benefit to colleges, which are hurting and closing, and potentially make campus based education more affordable.

- Create more rural and small city development zones, with national and state assistance, to benefit from economic development efforts.

- Provide childcare assistance so that people can work.

- Provide education at affordable rates, close to home and online, so that people can realistically get the education they need to remain in jobs in their areas.

- Create economic and education development zones in city areas of poverty, which will eventually eliminate the poverty and problems. Development grants would help.

- Create a national healthcare plan that prevents healthcare from ruining people economically. "Your money or your life" should never be a choice.

- With 100% employment, the job market will become more competitive, driving up all wages.

- Use the elasticity of the money supply to encourage growth.

- Lend money at very low interest to product development organizations.

- Provide similar assistance to other countries on programs that work.

No State is the same in its ability to fund programs or supervise them. Identical requirements can't apply to them all. But with economic development heads supervising this, most of these problems can be resolved and the US can again become a land of opportunity and dreams.

How money supply elasticity supports growth

Not much of anything happens without money. Most entrepreneurial driven new products, and economic development takes money. It's worth paying over time with some interest to make it happen. The benefits are enormous compared to the cost.

Money is multiplied in our economy.

The first multiplier is simply spending that enables more spending. Investopedia explains it this way: "Example of Velocity of Money

"Consider an economy consisting of two individuals, A and B, who have $100 each. A buys a car from B for $100. Then B purchases a home from A for $90. B has kids and enlists A's help in adding new construction to his home. For his efforts, B pays A $100. A also sells the car he bought from B back to him for $90. Thus, both parties in the economy have made transactions worth $400, even though they only possessed $100 each. This multiplication in the value of goods and services exchanged is made possible through the velocity of money in an economy."

So unlike with our own budgets where we have limited funds, the more money we spend into the economy, the more the economy expands.

The second multiplier is bank loans. When money is loaned out, it gets redeposited so that the deposit is available to make more loans. Some of a deposit is required to be held in reserve (reserve banking), and the rest can be loaned out as long as the bank shows equivalent assets and loans on its balance sheet. This can multiply money in the economy by up to 10x, depending on how much the

Fed requires in reserve. Since the Great Recession the Fed requires banks to keep more money on reserve, so the multiplier is less than 10x.

Consumer spending can be assisted by bank loans, however repayment eats into the money the consumer has for discretionary spending in the future. Discretionary spending drives the economy. So this stimulus can become a problem. Consumer borrowing is now at a higher rate than before 2007 and the Great Recession because people are having to borrow money just to stay even.

The third multiplier is the Keynesian Multiplier. That is, government spending will bring about cycles of growth. That multiplier is thought to be around 1.5%. The government is simply an extension of the consumer. The opposite is reflected in what happens during recessions and periods of austerity. Cutting government spending deepens the depth and length of recessions.

The Federal Reserve lending interest rates to Reserve Banks, other banks, and wealthy individuals, is currently near 0%. As a stimulus, it needs to target similar rates to universities, companies, and organizations that do product research and development to create new products and jobs. They provide great benefit to the economic future of individuals and the nation. While investors do a similar thing, helping choose and guide promising new businesses, they aren't in it to provide jobs, they're in it for personal profit (and often their own personal interests). Fewer jobs, more profit.

The economy isn't a pie in which there isn't enough good pieces for everyone. Our own spending creates the economy. Starve the economy with low wages and low spending, and we all starve. Feed the economy with higher wages and higher spending and we all benefit, including companies and investors. This is very hard to understand because it isn't intuitive. For more information on how our Federal Reserve and banking system work, see Appendix 3.

Toward economic participation for all

The stock market is used as a wealth building mechanism for wealthy people, and also for retirement plans. It's one of the distinguishing characteristics of Capitalism.

Does the stock market help the economy, or hinder it? It does both. Some new companies benefit by offering shares (IPLs), and in less developed countries the stock market is very helpful. But in the larger market, the stock market adds nothing substantial to the economy. It doesn't raise GDP. It doesn't add to workers' wages. In fact, wages followed increases in productivity up until around 1970, when this ceased.

Essentially what the stock market does is demand quarterly profits from companies, which causes them to sacrifice training, new product development, and long term investments that would improve company performance. To get new products, companies buy other companies and gut them of their products and employees. They're net job destroyers.

All investors care about is that the stock price goes up every quarter. On this they make a fortune. Unlike in the 1960s, employees no longer matter, nor do communities. Only shareholder profit is a concern. Wages don't go up. Wages have flatlined since 1970, only going up a few times since then.

Generally companies can simply get bank loans. Major banks are big enough to service their needs, and loans have the advantage of going away when paid, whereas stock goes on as a debt forever. So why do companies put up with this? Their CEOs and officers are rewarded in stock. Their guiding boards of directors represent shareholders. The obvious bias is to use stock. In reality, companies should buy back all of their stock and use loans.

Corporate raiders in the 1970s and 1980s bought companies that were barely surviving, sold off or stopped unprofitable product lines, and brought them back to life, often selling profitable portions to other companies. Their impact was both good and bad.

Corporations today buy healthy companies, take their technologies and markets, and abandon the rest, in what's termed "Merger Mania." This usually leaves many people unemployed after a year or two of transition to a new location.

Companies also close portions of their companies that aren't "profitable enough" to please investors.

Corporations are much less likely to invest in creating new products when they can simply buy another company's technology or product, and buy technology and products from entrepreneurs.

The net effect of corporations is to destroy jobs.

The stock market was responsible for two of the four major recessions of the last 20 years. In 2001 the Dot Com crisis came about because of "irrational exuberance," claimed then Federal Reserve Chairman Alan Greenspan. Greenspan was a major promoter of allowing businesses to police themselves. By the end of his term in office he had changed his mind on that. Anyway, the Dot Com promise of the 1990s, the bubble, popped when investors realized the software companies didn't have any markets for their new wares. The tech market crumbled.

I define investors irrationality as $I = \Delta^2$ Irrationality = change squared. The more the change in the stock market, the more irrational investors become. Only Circuit Breakers to stop trading on the market exchanges prevents certain destruction.

The Great Recession of the 2008 years was a major economic setback from which we have yet to recover, and recovery has been at great expense to our National Debt, which will have to be repaid. The current interest paid annually on the National Debt is $393.5 billion, which is 8.5% of our $4.45 trillion Federal Budget.

The debt is going up rapidly, and interest saps away money that could go for other things.

> In fiscal year 2021, interest will surpass the combined amount spent on Medicaid, the Children's Health Insurance Program, and subsidies for the purchase of health insurance under the Affordable Care Act.
>
> In fiscal year 2022, interest spending will exceed all mandatory spending other than that for Social Security and the major health care programs.lxxviii

The 2008 crisis was caused by several things. No one thought housing prices could go down. It just didn't happen. So in the hot market, lenders made loans to people who couldn't pay them, and underwriters signed off on the viability of those loans. Loan aggregators packaged them and sold them as substandard loans, but investors who purchased them didn't care. The market couldn't fail. And besides, they protected their gamble with Credit Default Swaps offered by investment services.

The house of cards fell. People couldn't pay their loans. When investors tried to use their Credit Default Swaps to get their money back, the large investments firms couldn't pay and it all fell apart. Investment firms quickly decided to become banks with FDIC protection. The economy went into a deep recession. This isn't the "business cycle" of ups and downs. Families again lost their jobs, homes, education, dreams because we let investors play fast and loose with our economy.

The stock market, while having no direct positive impact on the economy, repeatedly plunges us into recession. The government commonly uses austerity as a tool to get out of the recession, both deepening and prolonging it. We're a hot mess.

In analysis of the divisions we have in our society, the problems primarily are driven by economic fear and distress. In three major recessions in the first 20 years of this century, people have learned to live in far of losing their jobs, their homes, and their dreams. It's terrifying.

Solve economic loss and inequality, and most of the division simmers down and is manageable. (Sources are MIT and my own analysis of the last presidential election.) Economic inequality in rural areas, suburban areas where people are underpaid and losing jobs, and pockets of poverty, are tearing the nation apart. (On this, Trump was correct, but doesn't have the cures.)

A sign of change

Company CEOs are recognizing that this focus on increasing stockholder wealth at any cost simply transfers wealth from the bottom half of the population and kills off discretionary spending that fuels their companies.

> I often joke that you could divorce the stock market from companies and let investors simply gamble on companies doing well. There likely wouldn't be much difference for them.

This may change. The Business Roundtable, a group of CEOs of nearly 200 major U.S. corporations, issued a statement with a new definition of the "purpose of a corporation."

They reimagined corporations, as CNBC summarized, "Investing in employees, delivering value to customers, dealing ethically with suppliers and supporting outside communities are now at the forefront of American business goals."[lxxix]

Some MIT professors recommend that businesses enter into a new Social Contract with America, in which all Americans take part.

> Sadly I explored this idea of a Social Contract for years with a group and found that people don't trust the business world to turn away from greed. It's too ingrained. The only mandate businesses have is to make money, and making a fortune is an American Dream.
>
> Besides, it's systemic. Top CEOs are controlled by boards

representing investors, and mid- to small businesses generally scrape by and resent any interference in wages. Unions have been squeezed out. People want things put into laws.

This isn't just a US problem, it's a problem around the world.

Other mechanisms are being looked at to counter the problem of the nation's wage distribution hollowing out in the middle and sending huge numbers to the bottom. Most of these would have to be done by our Congress, and at this moment it's a moot question.

Wealth tax

This would be a higher tax rate on wealthy individuals. This tax right now is low, but it has been as high as 90%, which it was after WWII to resolve the nation's National Debt. While some wealthy individuals say they should have higher taxes, others say they shouldn't.

Tax on stock market gains

The stock market, and most corporations, made record profits all during the 2008 Great Recession years. The stock market can be a reliable way to fend off economic downfall. Especially since it causes it. But adding an additional tax would be double-taxing.

Tax on stock market transactions

I personally have explored this at length. I have had investors say to me that they will revolt at this paltry amount of .30 cents a trade, or .1% of the total trade, and take their investments out of the country. But the rest of the world would likely do the same tax, and countries could require that to do be headquartered in a country or do over 60% of its business in a country, the company would have to be listed on a stock exchange in that country. No more hiding in tax haven countries.

How would this work?

Most trades on the stock market are done automatically by computer. Investors aren't even involved. The NYSE annual trading volume is $1,314 trillion, for 907 billion shares. The tax revenue from just .1% trading volume would be $1.31 trillion a year.

Fifty percent of the US households on the bottom half of wage distribution number 130 million. If $1.31 trillion was divided among them, each would have $7700.00 more in income each year.

Looking at it another way, the amount needed to bring 63 million households to $50,000.00 would require $775 billion, more than covered by the $1.3 trillion. Household income for all could easily be boosted to $60,000.00.

At $60,000.00 household income, the incentive to work would remain, supplemental income would make each household economically viable for living expenses, education, and healthcare. Problems solved.

Everyone invested in company stock

This method would make everyone invested in their companies, and have stock market savings. The difficulties with this are that people tend to cash in their stock for things they need, and many companies don't offer stock. Although they could contribute to a 401K. But many small companies can't offer any benefits.

Insurance pool HSA

Why do people have to pay insurance companies huge sums to give them insurance coverage? It's simply profit for investors, pays huge unnecessary staffs, and is part of why we can't get medical costs down.

Households pay around $20,000.00 each year for different types of insurance. If each paid into an insurance pool for ten years, they could be self insured just as many companies are. Something to think about.

Labor Council

A council of business leaders and employees, could do the work of setting wages.

Conclusion to Toward a More Prosperous Economy For Everyone

In conclusion, it looks like people are getting sick and tired of being sick and tired. These may spread as other forms of social unrest as the Covid-19 pandemic takes its financial toll on families. In Israel the racial protests have turned to protests over the illegal annexation of the West Bank – one thing that stands in the way of peace with the Palestinians. The protests over racial oppression have gone around the world and may transform there as well. The Yellow Jacket protests in France indicate they are tired of economic oppression.

Likely all of the methods mentioned, and more, would bring economic equality back, to create a very prosperous US.

The time for change may be at hand. The moment is pregnant with possibilities that may bring us much needed change.

AI and Automation Impact on Economy Reference

Salesforce.com, *How the Future of AI will impact business. https://www.salesforce.com/blog/2019/04/future-of-ai-artificial-intelligence-business-impact.html.*

Automation potential of 750 US jobs, McKinsey Institute. https://public.tableau.com/profile/mckinsey.analytics#!/vizhome/AutomationandUSjobs/Technicalpotentialforautomation.

What the future of work will mean for jobs, skills, and wages, McKinsey Institute. https://www.mckinsey.com/featured-insights/future-of-work/jobs-lost-jobs-gained-what-the-future-of-work-will-mean-for-jobs-skills-and-wages#part2

Chapter 9: Generation Z – Everything is changing

Major demographic shifts bring changes in society. The Baby Boom generation brought changes in sexual attitudes. Millennials were labeled the "The Me Me Me Generation" for concentrating on themselves with no limits. "The incidence of narcissistic personality disorder is nearly three times as high for people in their 20s as for the generation that's now 65 or older, according to the National Institutes of Health"[lxxx]

A new era of women's empowerment brought us Me Too. Now Generation Z brings us probably the biggest changes of all. And the change works surprisingly well with work of the future.

There is no really sharp age division between Millennials and Generation Z. It's more of a metamorphosis but with growing sharp distinctions.

This short chapter covers not just working with Gen Z at work, but also in society's institutions, such as philanthropic organizations, with a special focus on religious groups. You will have to understand them to work with or educate them. In studying religion of the future, and looking ahead to government, Generation Z appears to be the coming agent of this change.

Generation Z has a new outlook on life

The backdrop to working with Generation Z (those born after 1995, now age 24 or so, is that according to an October 2019 Pew study, in 10 years, the percentage of people not identifying with religion increased 12% (very rapid decline), and those for whom religion is still an important part of their identity dropped to only

43%. Whites are the largest percentage leaving the church, while ethnic groups are more stable.

Religious attendance has been dropping since 1900, and accelerated after the year 2000. The acceleration seems almost exponential.

No individual is defined by their generation's statistics. We're all different. There may be differences between large city populations and rural, and between ethnicities. But these are central tendencies.

So, what is going on with Gen Z, and what does it mean?

For those Sadducees among us, who thought we just weren't being strict enough, sorry that has turned out not to be the problem. The stricter churches are experiencing the same decline. For those who think the world is ending because the church is shrinking, sorry, people are just as "spiritual" and in need as they ever were. They not only don't find what they need in the church, sadly they are repulsed by much of it. And for many of Gen Z it isn't even a thought.

While the trailing end of Millennials flummoxed researchers with their lack of enthusiasm for consumerism and going out the American way, Generation Z has a very different group of concerns, and they are rapidly becoming the largest group in a population experiencing stagnant growth. By 2030 we will have an equal number of people in all age ranges. The oldies but goodies are rapidly being replaced by Millennials and especially Generation Z.

Gen Z is very pragmatic. After watching their parents lose jobs and homes through two deep recessions, they want security and go after it. But they aren't necessarily big on college, which has priced itself out of reach. And that's okay because only around 35% of people need a full four year education for future jobs and good incomes.

Gen Z is very alarmed by school shootings, racism, violence in schools, homophobia, suppressing women, political alienation, and inequality. Ethics and equality are high on their list. Approval of LGBTQIA is at around 84% among young adults, and those disapproving are closely aligned with religious groups who oppose LGBTQIA.

Generation Z identifies as Christian only at around 66%. A third are atheists or don't identify with religion. Identifying with a religion doesn't mean that people actually practice it, and it's getting worse. Anecdotally, three people of the age 16 group have told me that their friends just aren't interested in religion or religious activity. It's a nonstarter.

This follows on the heels of several generations who have disaffiliated with the church. The primary reasons being, "Among the reasons Americans identified as important motivations in leaving their childhood religion are: they stopped believing in the religion's teachings (60%), their family was never that religious when they were growing up (32%), and their experience of negative religious teachings about or treatment of gay and lesbian people (29%).

Fewer than one in five Americans who left their childhood religion point to the clergy sexual-abuse scandal (19%), a traumatic event in their life (18%), or their congregation becoming too focused on politics (16%) as an important reason for disaffiliating." There is just too much dissonance to resolve between the God who sends everyone to Hell for an eternity of punishment and who is wrathful toward those who are different, and the God of love who has a way to bring everyone to heaven. They can't coexist, and they don't demonstrate a father's love. And this type of church mission isn't something they want involved in or can even believe in. For those inside and outside the church, this is the impression they receive either from the church or from the media. Yet the majority still believe in God.

Generation Z is very skeptical, independent, and they prefer to be entrepreneurs who invent and start businesses themselves. In other words, self-reliant, yet surprisingly social.

Gen Z is very inclusive. Being exclusive is a foreign idea that doesn't occupy a space in their minds. They reject it when they see it.

Generation Z, if they are religious, want the church to be more Christlike and less church-like.

Gen Z often delays marriage until their 30s, or don't get married at all. This includes the trailing end of the Millennials as a growing trend. This has a major impact on church attendance because attendance is very clearly associated with marriage and family. On average they remain in their parent's home until age 27 and on average marry around age 27.

Gen Z is spiritual. Like most of us they want to feel part of something greater than themselves and a higher purpose. They are more spiritual than religious. "Notably, most Americans who are classified as spiritual but not religious still identify with a religious tradition, even if they are less likely to attend services or say religion is important in their lives." Music is often a noted spiritual experience. "Some of the so-called nones are more like religious "alls" because they mix and match rituals from multiple faith groups."

Gen Z customers respond to edgy and visual marketing tactics. Videos—especially short ones like those created via the social network Vine—work particularly well with young customers.

Gen Z identity: "For Gen Zers, the key point is not to define themselves through only one stereotype but rather for individuals to experiment with different ways of being themselves and to shape their individual identities over time. In this respect, you might call them "identity nomads.""

Engaging Generation Z requires knowing them

What is Gen Z interested in? Meaningful social change. The exact things they are alarmed about. And they want to design the solutions. Community is very important to them. Face to face as well as digital media (including virtual) are important to them.

Gen Z wants to co-create culture, and they do. They are active participants, both using and shaping.

> Only one third of young adults feel deeply cared for by others. Connection is missing.
> - Barna.com

Getting people engaged involves three things

"... research found that there are three types of psychological benefits that are key to driving ... engagement:

- Functional benefits, or things a person wants to accomplish or do

- Emotional benefits, the way that people want to feel

- Identity benefits, or the way a person wants to be"

This corresponds very well with what I recently learned in an MIT course on the future of work. People want to be fully engaged. And this entrepreneurship and creativity will be very important to creating jobs of the future and the economy.

This also corresponds to what this age group says is missing in the church. Many want to feel connected with God, and they want a more spiritual life. This means being experiential, requiring both knowledge and action. Religion is participatory. It isn't just an intellectual experience for most.

This also corresponds with my own long experience in management. People want to be an active part of something, not an dangling appendage.

ITA Group indicated about organizations: "Help Create Connections Between People"

Workplace loneliness is real and a challenge for many companies. While you can't force your employees to be friends, you can set up an environment that encourages employees to connect.

Employee resource groups, interest clubs, coffee or lunch meet-ups, networking groups, mentorships, volunteer opportunities or company celebrations are just a few ways you can help foster connections among team members.

And the benefits are staggering: connection is so important, in fact, that its impact on your employees is greater than a boost in salary. Studies show that if you have a friend that you see on most days (especially at work), it's like earning $100,000 more each year."

And from decades of management experience, the opposite of this is certainly true. One bad apple makes everyone miserable and not want to come to work or be in an organization. They destroy the organization. It only takes one with a bad attitude. And for many churches they have one or more who have bad attitudes about others or their way of life.

Attracting Young Adults

Churches teaching spiritual practices were twice as likely to have a significant number of young adult participants.

While the style of music and technology is no clear indicator (both adults and young adults have preferences for either traditional or modern), the presence of a guitar and projector screens was correlated with higher young adult attendance.

Past studies have looked at young adult presence in congregations which are older on average and found they are not comfortable there. It's a consideration, especially if they are not engaged. Dying churches die. Seems harsh, but some churches seem to have a life cycle, unless they have high attendance (over 400).

Congregations that reported high spiritual vitality were three times as likely to have a significant number of young adults. (No change here for decades.)

Congregations reporting many programs for young adults were nearly twice as likely to have significant young adult participation as those reporting few or some programs.

It's less about the actual programs than the emphasis. Congregations that reported the greatest emphasis on young adult ministry, were twice as likely to also report engaging a significant number of young adults.

Summary of what organizations can do

Organizations can have a major role in helping Generation Z, if it accepts that role.

The church should be a place that serves the people, not a place that demands service to it.

It can facilitate the human connection and making friends for this generation.

It can help enable a platform or organization for social action.

It can facilitate in the experiential spiritual experience, and being connected to God, that they want,.

In many ways the church is, and always has been, about connecting with community, with peers, and with God.

It's very important to young adults that they have programs expressly for them.

Go out of their way to Attract young adults.

Special section for churches – From a former pastor, current minister

The role of the church

Churches choose different roles or spiritual emphasis for themselves. Some feel the Great Commission is their driving force and primary activity. Jesus told eleven apostles to spread the Good News, and the early churches had some evangelists who also did this. Others see that living out the Good News in their lives is their testimony to others.

The role of a church can be very varied. The Good News is mentioned in several verses in the Bible, which help clarify the width and breadth of it.

Teaching and exploration in the context of the Good News

The Good News changed the spiritual emphasis from sin to love and acceptance. The Good News message is demonstrated in the way shown by Christ (all Bible verses on the Good News considered).

It's an entry gate into the Kingdom of God that is among us, that is open to all without preconditions.

The Good News breaks down barriers between people, between people and God, and between people and a fulfilling (abundant) life. It involves us in creating a better world. Once unleashed, the human creative spirit can't be silenced.

Our answer is God. God's answer is us. Together we make the world a better place.

What is the Good News?

The church community offers so much, yet Jesus and the Apostles were sent to tell the Good News, and our lives are witness to it. At first this seems to be a mismatch of purposes.

What is the width and breadth of the Good News? Just preaching?

The disparity was caused by wondering what would we legitimately offer people that might be attractive and meaningful to them.

Forgiveness of sins, which was a major thing in Jesus time among the Jews, was a huge burden to many. Jewish happiness and meaning came from obeying the 613 Laws of God. But that explanation is simplistic. Jesus also talked about abundant life for his followers.

Jesus offered a different perspective, showing that the laws were made for man, not God who has no real needs. The prophets of Israel had previously expressed, and so did Jesus, that obeying laws didn't absolve you from helping others.

With reference to all passages in the Bible about Good News:

The Good News is an entry gate into the Kingdom of God that is among us. It breaks down barriers between people, between people and God, and between people and a fulfilling (abundant) life.

We have barriers of doing wrong to others, and the way Jesus showed us breaks down those barriers.

We have barriers over differences. The Kingdom is open to everyone.

We have barriers from pursuing things in life that aren't fulfilling. The Kingdom offers meaning, purpose, and fulfillment through activity with others. This is the part the church needs to focus on for attracting people. It can be supportive in people finding fulfillment that has many dimensions, not just worship.

Following are the verses referenced, and a summary:

Jesus said, ""I must preach the good news of the kingdom of God to the other cities also; for I was sent for this purpose.""

Luke 8:1: "Soon afterward he went on through cities and villages, preaching and bringing the good news of the kingdom of God."

Luke 16: 15-16: "But he said to them, "You are those who justify yourselves before men, but God knows your hearts; for what is exalted among men is an abomination in the sight of God. "The law and the prophets were until John; since then the good news of the kingdom of God is preached, and every one enters it violently [great force, emotional intensity]."

Acts 8:12: "they believed Philip as he preached good news about the kingdom of God and the name of Jesus Christ, they were baptized, both men and women."

Acts 10:34-42: "And Peter opened his mouth and said: "Truly I perceive that God shows no partiality, but in every nation any one who fears him and does what is right is acceptable to him. You know the word which he sent to Israel, preaching good news of peace by Jesus Christ (he is Lord of all)," ... "To him all the prophets bear witness that every one who believes in him receives forgiveness of sins through his name.""

Acts 14: 15: "... bring you good news, that you should turn from these vain things to a living God who made the heaven and the earth and the sea and all that is in them."

Summary, Good News is:

- The Kingdom of God is here (no longer separated by doing wrong).

- The Kingdom of God is for everyone.

- Forgiveness of sins for the asking.

- Meaningful activity, not useless or vanity.

Sources used in this chapter

https://www.itagroup.com/insights/things-know-about-generation-z

https://religionnews.com/2018/12/10/religion-declining-in-importance-for-many-americans-especially-for-millennials/

https://www.pewforum.org/2019/10/17/in-u-s-decline-of-christianity-continues-at-rapid-pace/?utm_source=Pew+Research+Center&utm_campaign=d8dae 17adc-

EMAIL_CAMPAIGN_2019_10_17_01_06&utm_medium=email
&utm_term=0_3e953b9b70-d8dae17adc-399956381

https://religionnews.com/2018/06/26/why-millennials-are-really-leaving-religion-its-not-just-politics-folks/

https://www.vox.com/identities/2017/11/10/16630178/study-spiritual-but-not-religious

https://www.patheos.com/blogs/jesuscreed/2014/05/17/white-millennials-are-leaving-the-church/

https://www.religionlink.com/source-guides/50-experts-on-the-evolving-religious-landscape/

https://www.prri.org/research/prri-rns-poll-nones-atheist-leaving-religion/

https://www.barna.com/research/disciple-next-generation/

https://www.visioncritical.com/blog/generation-z-infographics

https://religionnews.com/2018/12/06/reaching-generation-z-a-how-not-to-guide-for-churches/

https://www.itagroup.com/insights/baby-boomers-gen-z-what-know-about-employee-disengagement-across-generations-workplace

https://www.mckinsey.com/industries/consumer-packaged-goods/our-insights/true-gen-generation-z-and-its-implications-for-companies

Appendix 1: 2016 Wage Requirements for two person families

What does it cost for a family of two to live in the modern world (US)?

857.00 Apartment Rent for 1 or 2 bedroom

200.00 Average cost of apartment utilities per month (Zillow)

45.00 Internet

70.00 Cell phone family plan with 2 phones

200.00 Car payment on $11,000.00, 5 yr., 4 years old, 50,000 mi.

100.00 Car maintenance

150.00 Car insurance (conservative)

83.00 Gasoline (12,000 miles/yr., 30 MPG, 2.50/gal.

373.00 Thrifty food budget for two, depending on area. $500 would be much better.

117.00 One college online class (350.00, 1 semester, 2 people, 6 mo. = 117/mo.

200.00 ACA subsidized health insurance (Can be over 1000 for some plans). Subject to double-digit inflation.

268.00 Clothing. Sox wear out.

116.00 Home furnishings. First year is double.

250.00 Misc. parking, repairs, sex, fun, etc.

67.00 Retirement 2% of gross

295.00 Fed. tax 15% after 12,700 deduction

3391.00 Average total for two people, 41,088.00/yr., 20/hr., 10/hr. each.

5700.00 in high cost of living areas, 68,400.00/yr., 33.53/hr., 16.76/hr. Each.

Above requires a household income of 41,000 - 68,000.00.

38% of households earn below $38,000.00

The distribution indicates the majority of the people earning below $38,000.00, earned between $12,000 to 32,000.00

Around 47% of families fall into the below $40,320 to $54,884.00 EITC payment group, depending on dependents and other factors.

The problem we have can clearly be seen. Macroeconomic analysis leads to huge misimpressions. Too many people don't make nearly enough money. Minimum wage needs to be from $10 to 17.00/hr. to avoid people living in poverty and requiring massive government subsidies to exist.

Notes:

$1,638 Rent for 1 or 2 bedroom, if you can find one. SmartAsset.com

Assume some expenses are or can be government subsidized.

Assume TV by antenna and Internet. Internet is necessary for job search, communications, etc. No cable TV service.

Assume smart shopping for Internet service.

NYC cost of living is 68% higher than the US average

A used car will commonly cost at least $100.00 per month in maintenance costs. Can be much higher as the car gets older and has higher mileage. Younger buyers with lesser credit ratings may have to pay more in interest.

Some families may need two cars for work. Public transportation may not be available.

A food budget of $373.00 may not be a healthy diet and may be heavy in carbohydrates, leading to diabetes and weight problems.

Home furnishings, new or used: TV 800, couch 250, bed (mattress) 800, kitchen table 800, Dishes 150. assume ongoing yearly budget of half 1400.00

Rents have gone higher in recent years and apartments are very hard to find in many areas. In some areas people can find rent or gov. subsidized rent for 600, but this is rare.

Those with disadvantages become a burden on society. The number of government programs aimed at making their life and their kids' lives livable, are substantial and we pay for them. Start with EITC which is a once a year payment to those who work, based on their federal income tax and number of dependents. It goes to 24 million households and the average is over $3000.00. If they don't have health insurance, hospitals jack up the rates for the rest of us to cover their care. School lunches. Medicaid. Rent support. On and on.

Just under half of US households don't pay any Federal Income Tax.

What if there is a better way than creating dependents?

Help those who don't have the wherewithal to get better employment, to do so.

This takes the burden of supporting them off of us. It makes them financial contributors to our society so that there is more money for improving roads, schools, etc.

Reference

2016 Income Quintiles - Household income

From 2000 to 2017, US real income per capita has held steady.

Note in the graph for the highest quintile, the steady upward trend from 1970 on.

Note that for the other four quintiles, the steady downward trend.

Median household income was $59,000.00.

Those in the 25 to 34 age group earned average.

Those in the 15 to 24 age group earned $42,000.00

Wages for the lowest wage earners has only increased 32 cents an hour in 40 years.

(According to the Economic Policy Institute, half of wage earners earned $40,000.00 a year in 2019, if they worked full time.)

38% of households earn below $38,000.00

The wage distribution indicates the majority of the people earning below $38,000.00, earned between $12,000 to 32,000.00

Working families with children that have annual incomes below about $40,320 to $54,884 earn EITC. The average EITC was $3,176, boosting wages by about $265 a month, in a single payout from tax forms. EITC was paid to 26 Million families, lifting about 5.8 million people out of poverty, including about 3 million children.

Around 47% of families fall into the below $40,320 to $54,884.00 group, depending on dependents and other factors.

So while macroeconomic averages tell the story of US wage growth, it doesn't drill down into the details of what typical families face, which is a continuously shrinking share of US income, and difficulty having the money to do things that are necessary.

Median individual income for all earners in the workforce was $37,610.00

References:

https://www.statista.com/statistics/203247/shares-of-household-income-of-quintiles-in-the-us/

https://en.wikipedia.org/wiki/Household_income_in_the_United_States

https://www.cbpp.org/research/federal-tax/policy-basics-the-earned-income-tax-credit

Appendix 2: Courses taken the first two years of college

The first two years of college are usually centered on core education classes. These classes include **English, math, science, history and foreign language**, and they introduce students to different paths of study. It is best for students to take these classes immediately after graduating from high school to avoid having to take remedial classes later to refresh their memories. The core education classes students take during their freshman year will provide a solid foundation for the more advanced courses related to their selected majors.

Humanities Classes

Humanities classes consist of studying philosophy, religion, the arts and literature. They are good classes to take during freshman year due to their challenging content. Students enrolled in humanities classes will receive a well-rounded education of the world. Furthermore, knowledge gained from taking humanities classes provides them with the ability to converse intelligently in any academic major.

Colleges typically require 3 to 8 credits of natural science, including subjects like:

- Chemistry.
- Biology.
- Anatomy and physiology.
- Ecology.
- Geology.
- Environmental science.
- Astronomy.
- Physics.

Math: Most degrees require 3-6 math credits, although math-intensive degrees will require more. Courses that fit into this category include:

- Algebra - (Other titles could include College Algebra, Intro to Algebra, or Foundations of Algebra)
- Geometry
- Calculus
- Trigonometry
- Statistics
- Quantitative analysis

Natural Science: Science is much more than rock collecting or the domain of geeks. As the study of the natural world, it gives us a framework for safely and creatively interacting with the matter that surrounds us. Colleges typically require 3 to 8 credits of natural science, including subjects like:

- Chemistry
- Biology
- Anatomy and physiology
- Ecology
- Geology
- Environmental science
- Astronomy
- Physics
- Oceanography

Social Sciences: Social sciences give us insight into who humans are and how we interact with one another. As the study of human groups, social sciences encompass:

- Psychology
- Sociology
- Anthropology
- History
- Economics

- Political science

- Government

- Geography

Humanities: Culture is a huge part of civilization, so every well-educated person needs a little insight into how people express themselves in a culture. With such a broad range of subjects, colleges vary widely on what constitutes "humanities," but often include courses on:

- Art

- Music

- Communication

- Speech

- Philosophy

- Religion

- Literature

- Ethics

- Languages

- History (rarely)

Diversity: A newcomer to Gen Ed requirements, diversity courses teach students to value other cultures and beliefs. Depending on the school, diversity courses may include:

- Religion

- Cultural diversity

- Social responsibility

- World religions (also a humanities subject)

Source: https://education.seattlepi.com/good-classes-freshman-year-college-1139.html

Appendix 3 – How the banking system works

The US doesn't "print money," except to meet the minimal demand for cash. "Printing money" is a myth. The monetary processes in the US are complex, but understandable.

How banks work

Banks loan money from deposits they have, and can loan against their other equity such as the properties they own. Deposits and property are on one side of the balance sheet. Lending is on the other side of the balance sheet, and the two sides have to remain balanced.

Banks can't loan more money than they have on the equity side of their balance sheet.

> Banks can borrow money from the Federal Reserve overnight to help with shortfalls, but this is made up the next day with deposits.

Banks regain money through loan payments, selling their loans to others, and through additional deposits.

Here's the cool parts that make money expansion possible. Banks sell their loans to investors for more money than they loaned out. That adds to the equity side of their balance sheet.

Secondly, loans to others are redeposited to the same or other banks until their full amount is used. Every time someone takes out a loan, they deposit the money somewhere. Each time a loan is redeposited, it adds to some bank's equity. This is a multiplication factor for money.

> Banks can only loan a portion of their equity. For the safety of the banking system, a portion of their money is required to be held in reserve. This amount is set by the Federal Reserve.

The Federal Reserve system

The US Treasury and the Federal Reserve are two entirely different systems. They are often confused.

Money that is paid to the US Government goes into the US Treasury. Money the Government spends comes out of the US Treasury. Money that the government borrows to pay its debts, such as government bonds, comes into the US Treasury.

Most money is virtual. It's in banks. If there is insufficient physical money to meet everyday needs, the Treasury can print more. But it doesn't print money to help the economy.

The Federal Reserve system is responsible for the US banking system. Congress requires the Fed to ensure high employment and control inflation. The Fed does these things by heating up or cooling the economy through lending and interest rates. It tightens or improves the money supply.

What is the magic the Fed uses to accomplish these tasks? It controls the basic interest rates for lending to banks, and it lends to members of the Federal Reserve system, which are mostly regional reserve banks which lend to mainstream banks. When base interest rates get higher, demand for regular bank loans decreases. And vice versa. These actions control the "money supply."

The Federal Reserve lends money with interest, so it makes money. The interest provides it revenue for lending. The Fed holds its revenue in reserve. Excess revenue beyond a certain amount is turned over to the US Treasury. Currently Congress mandates that money for infrastructure spending.

General References

A wide range of authoritative references, noted in the End Notes, were used in preparing these white papers. My thanks to the MIT course, *The Future of Work: Preparing for Disruption,* and a similar World Bank course, which filled in the gaps in my knowledge for this 13 year research that I was already doing. My research included a large amount of material from MIT, Harvard, Georgetown University, and other universities.

You would expect leading universities dedicated to technology and business, with major initiatives in the field, to have an excellent grasp of this subject. In using my notes I've tried to avoid using university course material, but instead find other similar sources.

Brookings Institute and McKinsey Institute, which have been very informative on these topics for many years, are major sources of technology and labor studies, and also strongly informed these papers, starting from many years ago.

Lumina Communications and *The Hechinger Report* were excellent sources of articles and resources used in researching these subjects. Shout out to them for their excellent work.

There is no liberal or conservative thought in these papers, or animosity toward colleges or States. These comments are simply pragmatic, dealing with the major issues of today.

Author's Note

My primary interest is in helping our young adults be prepared by our educational system for the future of work and life, helping those being displaced in their jobs by technology achieve the education for new jobs, and helping rural, mid-American, and worldwide communities restored to economically viable areas.

About the Author

Dorian Scott Cole is a communicator by profession, with education and direct experience in technology, business management, psychology, religion, radio announcing, acting, and as a field engineer, having had full careers in several fields. He worked as a senior development analyst for Writers Workshop, L.A. He teaches writing and acting in independent settings, and has been the author of several Websites since 1996.

He produced entertainment videos through his company, Movie Stream Productions. His production series, STL Comedy (similar to SNL), included 22 professional actors, and 10 writers.

Dorian Cole Biography

Dorian is a proven technology, business management, training, course development, writing, marketing and product manager, and video production professional, with over 20 years in business management.

He studied economics off and on since 2007 to avoid be misled by politicians. These studies included leading thinkers in the field on macroeconomics, and most recently microeconomics through MIT, as well as his own research. His articles have been used by insurance companies.

In entertainment production, early in his career he studied radio at SIU then was a radio announcer at regional station WTAY. He later studied video production at the Broadcast Center. He studied acting at College of DuPage. Later in life he began movie production of STL Comedy episodes, and continues to edit video.

He was educated in electronics in the US Navy. Then took electrical engineering and biomedical engineering courses while at two electrical power industries and then as a medical field engineer. In the Navy, the electrical power industry, and medical research and clinical, he worked with high tech equipment and was often assigned design projects.

He attended EIU and IU in psychology and religious studies while a pastor at two churches and a counselor, and was a member of the Spencer, Indiana Association of Psychologists. He worked with corporate culture and mission change at DuPont and Enkia, and studies and works with attitude change in a number of settings.

At DuPont, once Fortune 10 in the US, he hired and developed employees from DeVry, Ivy Tech, and universities. He made financial budgets and forecasts for the Midwest medical division. Responsible for regional Profit and Loss, he gained major increases in revenue and operating efficiency. He was also charged with world field sales training.

While at DuPont he was a field engineer who investigated accidents and equipment failures that local technicians couldn't resolve. He re-developed a thirteen week technology course, reduced it to three weeks, added two more units for new medical equipment, and instructed foreign students who struggled with English. It was considered more effective than the original course.

Also at DuPont, he was handed another Midwest medical division to manage which had major employee and customer relations problems. He had the problems straightened out in two weeks through business and attitude changes that involved people in outcomes, and this remained calm for the duration of his management.

When the medical division went up for sale, Dorian changed to technical and marketing writing, and then worked for four high tech companies, became a marketing manager for two, and a product manager for another. At the fourth, which was on the Georgia Tech campus and which developed artificial intelligence for business, he worked with corporate culture and changed the company focus from sales to strategic marketing. He was also active in finding a buyer for that company.

Through helping his contractor brother on high end building projects in commercial and residential buildings, he passed the Internachi inspector test in 2017. He has redesigned commercial buildings for MRI and CT installations, and has designed and built some houses. Appropriate engineers were involved as needed.

Since 1990 Dorian's company, TechGenie Media, contracted work with clients needing focus groups, video editing of seminars, streaming, TV programs, and editing of commercials. He has over fifteen years experience with focus groups.

He publishes the Web sites Movie Stream Productions, Visual Writer, and One Spirit Resources.

He worked with one credit card company to achieve more secure Internet access, and developed and programmed a TV streaming site, streaming from ABC-Disney servers. Security was bank level. At times he developed and taught courses in acting, writing, and Internet technology.

He was senior development analyst for Writers Workshop in L.A. for over ten years. His book *How To Write A Screenplay* was used as a non-curriculum addition in L.A. and other schools, which he converted to a hypertext self-teaching format, and is still available. He is also the author of *Writers Workshop Script Doctor*. He has several fiction and nonfiction books published, and has movie credits in Producing, Writing, Directing, Art, and Editing.

He has created and presented courses in technology, sales, writing, and acting.

His nonfiction books include *The Prophetic Pattern: Discussion Guide for Ancient and Modern Prophecy*, and *Ontology of God: The voices of the ancients speak*, which is comprehensive research into the development of ancient law, mercy, and love in many religions. His technology white papers were used in many companies, including incorporated into IBM's white papers.

Other books by this author

My specialty in fiction is the relatively quick read for business travelers and those who either don't like long books or don't have time to read them.

Woman Tames Cretin play and screenplay is available as a play (and screenplay for student and other productions).

Death By Christmas: Be Kind Or It May Kill You. Comedy. An unscrupulous, greedy lawyer, blunders into Christmas with the wrong attitude in this lighthearted romp. A nitwit lawyer, and maybe the Grim Reaper, usher Fenrick through a series of humorous, life threatening events.

Liars Truth. Too Stupid To Live series. Drama. A corrupt governor dies in a fit of stupidity. He is uncertain of his life standing, so journeys in Hell, where he feels he doesn't belong. Given a second chance, he is assigned to find damaged and lost, but wonderfully colorful souls in Hell, from any time period, who might redeem themselves through a second chance, and bring them into situations to better themselves.

How To Write A Screenplay. A guide for beginning writers. Writers Workshop basic guide, Edition 3. Designed as a fun, basic guide to get writers writing their screenplays immediately. This covers the basics of plot, characters, dialogue, and screenplay format. It was designed by Dorian Scott Cole, a development analyst, for Writers Workshop, L.A. in their program for high schools, with printing assistance from the American Film Institute.

Unauthorized Access. Dion's Enigmas™ series. Legal mystery, action, romance. A chance encounter in a lounge gets Dion involved with a "come here, get away" new girl friend. She's an ex-police detective who seems to have a warehouse full of problems. She is running because of a death threat from her corrupt husband, who could attack her at any time.

She involves Dion in interrelated cases in which an injured veteran is accused of hacking, and his friend is accused of vehicular homicide. "Of course" both are innocent, even though they hide multiple secrets protecting others, that Dion must unravel.

Nowhere Man: A psychiatrist confronts a mysterious pandemic that is invading a town, with bizarre effects on those afflicted, and no cure in sight.

Total Immersion: New adults. A young man becomes lost in virtual reality, but a young woman helps him find his way out.

Connect with Dorian Scott Cole

I really appreciate your reading my book! Here are my social media coordinates:

Dorian Cole on Facebook:
https://www.facebook.com/dorian.cole.391

Visit my websites:

VisualWriter.com, with *Nations Agenda,* including the series, *The Future Project.* Inquiry and commentary on the how, what, and challenges of writing and life. For movie makers, novelists, nonfiction writers, journalists. Since 1996.

OneSpiritResources.com: Spirituality and religion.

MovieStreamProductions.com/msp_insider/ Movie Production.

Footnotes

- [i] *Timeline of historic inventions,* Wikipedia - https://en.wikipedia.org/wiki/Timeline_of_historic_inventions#Earliest_inventions

[ii] Robert W. Fogel. *Catching Up with the Economy.* American Economic Review, 89 (1): 1-21. *Stagnation or exponential growth — considering two economic futures,* Louis D. Johnston | 2014 https://www.minnpost.com/macro-micro-minnesota/2014/11/stagnation-or-exponential-growth-considering-two-economic-futures/

[iii] *Fourth Industrial Revolution,* World Economic Forum - https://www.weforum.org/focus/fourth-industrial-revolution

[iv] Marc S. Tucker, Betsy Brown Ruzzi. *Message To America.* National Center On Education and the Economy. http://ncee.org/wp-content/uploads/2019/06/NCEE-PolicyBrief-on-MD-FINAL.pdf

[v] James Fallows and Deborah Fallows. *Our Towns.*

[vi] Mark Muro, Robert Maxim, and Jacob Whiton, *Automation and Artificial Intelligence: How machines are affecting people and places,* https://www.brookings.edu/research/automation-and-artificial-intelligence-how-machines-affect-people-and-places/

[vii] MARK MURO, JACOB WHITON, and ROBERT MAXIM, *WHAT JOBS ARE AFFECTED BY AI?* 2019. Metropolitan Policy Program at Brookings. https://www.brookings.edu/wp-content/uploads/2019/11/2019.11.20_BrookingsMetro_What-jobs-are-affected-by-AI_Report_Muro-Whiton-Maxim.pdf#page=11 Mark Muro, Jacob Whiton, and Robert Maxim. *REPORT: What jobs are affected by AI?* Better-paid, better-educated workers face the most exposure. 2019. https://www.brookings.edu/research/what-jobs-are-affected-by-ai-better-paid-better-educated-workers-face-the-most-exposure/?utm_campaign=Metropolitan%20Policy%20Program&utm_source=hs_email&utm_medium=email&utm_content=80415838

[viii] OLGA KHAZAN, *Work From Home Is Here to Stay,* 2020. The Atlantic. https://www.theatlantic.com/health/archive/2020/05/work-from-home-pandemic/611098/

[ix] Shirin Ghaffary, *Facebook is the latest major tech company to let people*

work from home forever, 2020. Vox. https://www.vox.com/recode/2020/5/21/21266570/facebook-remote-work-from-home-mark-zuckerberg-twitter-covid-19-coronavirus

x   Jessica Snouwaert, *54% of adults want to work remotely most of the time after the pandemic, according to a new study from IBM,* 2020. Business Insider. https://www.businessinsider.com/54-percent-adults-want-mainly-work-remote-after-pandemic-study-2020-5

xi   Andrew Chamings, *2 out of 3 tech workers would leave SF permanently if they could work remotely,* 2020. SF Gate. https://www.sfgate.com/living-in-sf/article/2-out-of-3-tech-workers-would-leave-SF-15289316.php?fbclid=IwAR1lZS_SCYg4qCMX24iKmk-SSPsx5FbRpjmzCcl77NREMVJohLK6C4PmBJo

xii   Georgetown University, J*ob Growth and Education Requirements Through 2020,* https://cew.georgetown.edu/cew-reports/recovery-job-growth-and-education-requirements-through-2020/

xiii   Kimberly Amadeo, *Consumer Spending Trends and Current Statistics.* The Balance, https://www.thebalance.com/consumer-spending-trends-and-current-statistics-3305916

xiv   William R. Emmons, *Don't Expect Consumer Spending To Be the Engine of Economic Growth It Once Was,* Federal Reserve Bank of St. Louis. https://www.stlouisfed.org/publications/regional-economist/january-2012/dont-expect-consumer-spending-to-be-the-engine-of-economic-growth-it-once-was

xv   Center On Budget And Policy Priorities, *Chart Book: Tracking the Post-Great Recession Economy.* https://www.cbpp.org/research/economy/chart-book-tracking-the-post-great-recession-economy

xvi   Associated Press reports *National Association for Business Economics Survey: Half of business economists see recession by 2020.* Associated Press. https://www.apnews.com/34de92d5464b4fa5844234bb78063fdb

xvii   Mark Muro, Robert Maxim, Jacob Whiton, *Automation and Artificial Intelligence: How machines are affecting people and places.* Brookings Institute. https://www.brookings.edu/research/automation-and-artificial-intelligence-how-machines-affect-people-and-places/

xviii   MIT course on *Shaping Work of the Future*

xix   ibid

xx   Anthony P. Carnevale, Nicole Smith, Jeff Strohl, *job Growth and Education Requirements Through 2020.* Georgetown University, Center on Education and the Workforce. https://cew.georgetown.edu/cew-reports/recovery-job-growth-and-education-requirements-through-2020/

xxi *Public Trust in Government: 1958-2019,* Pew Research Center, Public Policy and Politics. https://www.people-press.org/2019/04/11/public-trust-in-government-1958-2019/

xxii *Congress and the Public,* Gallup. https://news.gallup.com/poll/1600/congress-public.aspx

xxiii *Democracy in America,* Northwestern Institute for Policy Research. Benjamin Page. https://www.ipr.northwestern.edu/about/news/2018/page-democracy-in-america.html

xxiv Bob Eccles, *Investors Can And Should Address The Fundamental Causes Of Income Inequality.* Forbes.com. https://www.forbes.com/sites/bobeccles/2018/10/30/investors-can-and-should-address-the-fundamental-causes-of-income-inequality/#6f3c25d1ed51

xxv David Ruccio, *Graph of the week: USA productivity and real hourly wages 1964-2008.* Real World Economics Review Blog. [This common chart is available from multiple sources.] https://rwer.wordpress.com/2010/11/20/graph-of-the-week-usa-productivity-and-real-hourly-wages-1964-2008/

xxvi Steve Denning, *The Surprising Truth About Where New Jobs Come From.* Forbes. https://www.forbes.com/sites/stevedenning/2014/10/29/the-surprising-truth-about-where-new-jobs-come-from/#4614ea713382

xxvii Jason Wiens and Chris Jackson, *The Importance of Young Firms for Economic Growth.* Kauffman Foundation. https://www.kauffman.org/what-we-do/resources/entrepreneurship-policy-digest/the-importance-of-young-firms-for-economic-growth

xxviii *Congressional Research Service Calls Three Strikes on the Trump Tax Cuts.* Institute on Taxation and Economic Policy. https://itep.org/congressional-research-service-calls-three-strikes-on-the-trump-tax-cuts/

xxix Harvard Kennedy School for Business and Government, has its Social Responsibility Initiative. https://www.hks.harvard.edu/centers/mrcbg/programs/cri

xxx Alexandra Spiliakos, *WHAT DOES "SUSTAINABILITY" MEAN IN BUSINESS?* Harvard Business School, Business Insights. https://online.hbs.edu/blog/post/what-is-sustainability-in-business, xxxi *Business Roundtable Redefines the Purpose of a Corporation to Promote 'An Economy That Serves All Americans'.* https://www.businessroundtable.org/business-roundtable-redefines-the-purpose-of-a-corporation-to-promote-an-economy-that-serves-all-americans

xxxii Anders Melin and Jeff Green, *Devil is in details of CEOs' social pledge,* LA Times. https://enewspaper.latimes.com/infinity/article_share.aspx?guid=aa4f903f-3a03-4683-9f12-049a9c8d2958&fbclid=IwAR3A4_zJXy_RxwS9cLR-gq-OUn62Zl6es-Wi8eb4ITHGmxxNsjrMZJZ9200

xxxiii Bob Eccles, I*nvestors Can And Should Address The Fundamental Causes Of Income Inequality.* Forbes.com. https://www.forbes.com/sites/bobeccles/2018/10/30/investors-can-and-should-address-the-fundamental-causes-of-income-inequality/#6f3c25d1ed51

xxxiv *New Report: Why and How Investors Can Respond to Income Inequality.* TIIP: The Investment Integration Project. https://www.tiiproject.com/coming-soon-why-and-how-investors-can-respond-to-income-inequality/

xxxv *Recovery: job growth and education requirements through 2020.* Georgetown University Center on Education and the Workforce, 2020. https://cew.georgetown.edu/wp-content/uploads/2014/11/Recovery2020.ES_.Web_.pdf

xxxvi Elise Gould, *State of Working America Wages 2019.* 2020. Economic Policy Institute. https://www.epi.org/publication/swa-wages-2019/

xxxvii Nick Hanauer (Founder of the public-policy incubator Civic Ventures), *IDEAS: Better Schools Won't Fix America.* 2019. The Atlantic. https://www.theatlantic.com/magazine/archive/2019/07/education-isnt-enough/590611/?utm_source=The+Hechinger+Report&utm_campaign=6148284e9a-EMAIL_CAMPAIGN_WEEKLY_2019_06_18_03_04&utm_medium=email&utm_term=0_d3ee4c3e04-6148284e9a-322736177

xxxviii Elise Gould, Zane Mokhiber, and Julia Wolfe, *Class of 2018, College edition Report.* 2018. https://www.epi.org/publication/class-of-2018-college-edition/

xxxix Prestin Cooper, *Underemployment Persists Throughout College Graduates' Careers.* Forbes. 2018. https://www.forbes.com/sites/prestoncooper2/2018/06/08/underemployment-persists-throughout-college-graduates-careers/#b39cbc674907 xl Sibile Marcellus, *Underemployment for recent grads worse today than in early 2000s.* Yahoo Finance, 2019. https://finance.yahoo.com/news/underemployment-for-recent-grads-worse-today-than-in-early-2000-s-180429491.html

xli Nick Hanauer (Founder of the public-policy incubator Civic Ventures), *IDEAS: Better Schools Won't Fix America.* 2019. The Atlantic. https://www.theatlantic.com/magazine/archive/2019/07/education-isnt-enough/590611/?utm_source=The+Hechinger+Report&utm_campaign=614 8284e9a-
EMAIL_CAMPAIGN_WEEKLY_2019_06_18_03_04&utm_medium=emai l&utm_term=0_d3ee4c3e04-6148284e9a-322736177

xlii Reference: Tony Wagner, Senior Research Fellow and the Learning Institute, Harvard Innovation Lab. https://learningpolicyinstitute.org/person/tony-wagner , https://www.tonywagner.com/ , https://www.youtube.com/watch?v=hvDjh4l-VHo

xliii Thomas A. Kochan and Lee Dyer, *Shaping the Future of Work: A Handbook for Action and a New Social Contract,* (MITxPress, 2017)

xliv Devin Fidler. *Future skills, update and literature review,* prepared for Act Foundation, and the Joyce Foundation. Institute for the Future. PDF: https://www.iftf.org/fileadmin/user_upload/downloads/wfi/ACTF_IFTF_Fut ureSkills-report.pdf

xlv Jeffrey R. Young, *Did Students Learn As Much During Remote Online Instruction?* 2020. EDSURGE PODCAST. https://www.edsurge.com/news/2020-05-19-did-students-learn-as-much-during-remote-online-instruction

xlvi States can build a strong foundation for economic success and shared prosperity by investing in education. Providing expanded access to high quality education will not only expand economic opportunity for residents, but also likely do more to strengthen the overall state economy than anything else a state government can do. States can increase the strength of their economies and their ability to grow and attract high-wage employers by investing in education and increasing the number of well-educated workers.

Noah Berger and Peter Fisher, *A Well-Educated Workforce Is Key to State Prosperity,* Economic Policy Institute, https://www.epi.org/publication/states-education-productivity-growth-foundations/

xlvii Within 3 years of initial enrollment, about 30 percent of undergraduates in associate's and bachelor's degree programs who had declared a major had changed their major at least once. About 1 in 10 students changed majors more than once: 10 percent of associate's degree students and 9 percent of bachelor's   degree   students

Report: *Beginning College Students Who Change Their Majors Within 3 Years of Enrollment,* Data Point, US Department of Education, https://files.eric.ed.gov/fulltext/ED578434.pdf

xlviii Elyssa Kirkham, *Study: Here's How Much College Credits Actually Cost,* Student Loan Hero, Lending Tree. https://studentloanhero.com/featured/cost-per-credit-hour-study/

xlix Report: *Tuition and Fees and Room and Board over Time, College Board.* https://trends.collegeboard.org/college-pricing/figures-tables/tuition-fees-room-and-board-over-time

l US Gov. report: *How long does it take to pay off a student loan?* https://www.consumerfinance.gov/ask-cfpb/how-long-does-it-take-to-pay-off-a-student-loan-en-621/

li Forum: *Leveling the Playing Field: Policy Options to Improve Postsecondary Education and Career Outcomes,* The Hamilton Project.

lii Forecast: *The Budget and Economic Outlook: 2018 to 2028,* Congressional budget Office. https://www.cbo.gov/publication/53651

liii Group of 60 economists: *Economic Forecasting Survey*, Wall Street Journal. https://www.wsj.com/graphics/econsurvey/

liv Companies are less concerned about an economic slowdown. They are making more job cuts while simultaneously hiring, to apparently retool employees   for   changes   in   technology   and   growth.   The

[Note: The quantity of job postings is difficult to interpret. Many are forward looking and dependent on how the economy and markets perform, and may or   may   not   get   filled.]

Challenger, Gray & Christmas, Inc., Press Release: *2019 Hiring Outlook: 55 Percent of Companies Plan to Hire, Less Concern About the Economy,* https://www.challengergray.com/press/press-releases/2019-hiring-outlook-55-percent-companies-plan-hire-less-concern-about-economy

lv James Manyika, Susan Lund, Michael Chui, Jacques Bughin, Jonathan Woetzel, Parul Batra, Ryan Ko, and Saurabh Sanghvi, *Jobs lost, jobs gained: What the future of work will mean for jobs, skills, and wages,* McKinsey &

Company. https://www.mckinsey.com/featured-insights/future-of-work/jobs-lost-jobs-gained-what-the-future-of-work-will-mean-for-jobs-skills-and-wages

lvi James Manyika and Kevin Sneader, *AI, automation, and the future of work: Ten things to solve for.* McKinsey & Company. https://www.mckinsey.com/featured-insights/future-of-work/ai-automation-and-the-future-of-work-ten-things-to-solve-for.

lvii Justin Fox, Jay W. Lorsch, *What Good Are Shareholders?* Harvard Business Review. https://hbr.org/2012/07/what-good-are-shareholders

Dan W. Brock and Allen Buchanan, *Ethical Issues in For-Profit Health Care.* NIH National Center for Biotechnology Information. https://www.ncbi.nlm.nih.gov/books/NBK217902/

Joe Wallace and Akane Otani, Wall Street Journal. https://www.wsj.com/articles/investors-brace-for-hit-to-profits-as-costs-rise-11554283800

lviii James Manyika, Susan Lund, Michael Chui, Jacques Bughin, Jonathan Woetzel, Parul Batra, Ryan Ko, Saurabh Sanghvi, *Investors Brace for Hit to Profits as Costs Rise. Jobs Lost, Jobs Gained: Workforce Transitions In A Time Of Automation,* McKinsey Global Institute. https://www.mckinsey.com/~/media/mckinsey/featured%20insights/Future%20of%20Organizations/What%20the%20future%20of%20work%20will%20mean%20for%20jobs%20skills%20and%20wages/MGI-Jobs-Lost-Jobs-Gained-Report-December-6-2017.ashx

lix (Removed)

lx "… an increasing trade/GDP ratio is simply a reflection of greater specialisation. The fragmentation of production that is reflected in the expansion of GVCs also occurs domestically. If on net the global trade/GDP ratio levels off, there may well be substantial scope for continued fragmentation and specialisation within countries and regions."

Bernard Hoekman, *Has global trade peaked?* 2015. International Trade and Investment, World Economic Forum. https://www.weforum.org/agenda/2015/06/has-global-trade-peaked/

Dave Reifschneider, William L. Wascher, and David W. Wilcox, *Aggregate Supply in the United States: Recent Developments and Implications for the Conduct of Monetary Policy,* Finance and Economics Discussion Series, Divisions of Research & Statistics and Monetary Affairs, Federal Reserve

Board, Washington, D.C. https://www.federalreserve.gov/econresdata/feds/2013/files/feds201377r.pdf

lxi Eric Levitz, *Millennials Aren't Post-Consumerist, They're Just Poor, Fed Finds,* NY Mag, Intelligencer. http://nymag.com/intelligencer/2018/12/federal-reserve-millennials-study-arent-post-consumerist-theyre-just-poor.html

Deborah Weinswig, *Seismic Shift To Millennials Driving Dramatic Changes In U.S. Furniture Market,* https://www.forbes.com/sites/deborahweinswig/2016/02/15/seismic-shift-to-millennials-driving-dramatic-changes-in-us-furniture-market/#29b86f1a1cab

lxii Jennifer Ribarsky, Changku Kang and Esther Bolton, *The drivers of differences between growth in GDP and household adjusted disposable income in OECD countries,* [Organisation for Economic Co-operation and Development (OECD) countries, is an intergovernmental economic organisation with 36 member countries, founded in 1961 to stimulate economic progress and world trade], OECDiLibrary, https://www.oecd-ilibrary.org/economics/the-drivers-of-differences-between-growth-in-gdp-and-household-adjusted-disposable-income-in-oecd-countries_5jlz6qj247r8-en

lxiii Report, *Personal Income and Its Disposition,* US Bureau of Economic Analysis. https://apps.bea.gov/iTable/iTable.cfm?reqid=19&step=3&isuri=1&1921=survey&1903=58#reqid=19&step=3&isuri=1&1921=survey&1903=58

lxiv *Here's the Average American's Credit Card Debt -- and How to Get Yours Under Control,* Ascent Staff. Motley Fool. https://www.fool.com/the-ascent/credit-cards/blog/heres-the-average-americans-credit-card-debt-and-h/

lxv John Forsyth, Brian Schaitkin, Sumair Sayani, Ben Cheng, *CEO Briefs: Q3 US Consumer Demand and the Outlook for 2019.* The Conference Board and Nielsen, The Conference Board. https://www.conference-board.org/blog/postdetail.cfm?post=6912

lxvi Southern Regional Educational Board, reported on Diverse, Report: *Technology Advancements Causes Changes in American Workforce.* https://diverseeducation.com/article/138132/?fbclid=IwAR1k0r4hm2EVHZeI8Qz8I8LIoZKp-rLX3UBpC777OG06DMEqjRNr-tEOrgY

lxvii *Businesses partner with MIT.* https://executive.mit.edu/blog/partnering-with-universities-in-innovation-ecosystems-how-to-unlock-more-value Teaching + Learning Lab https://tll.mit.edu/

^{lxviii} *Resources, for online teaching. Every Learner Everywhere.* https://www.everylearnereverywhere.org/resources

^{lxix} Laura Ascione, Managing Editor, Content Services, *This new playbook helps faculty with best practices in online learning.* 2020. eCampus News. https://www.ecampusnews.com/2020/06/04/this-new-playbook-helps-faculty-with-best-practices-in-online-learning/?all

^{lxx} Jessica Gordon, *Building a Cooperative Solidarity Commonwealth.* 2016. https://thenextsystem.org/building-cooperative-solidarity-commonwealth?link_id=6&can_id=f49234a4ca1ad857cbf2f5b146c76b37&source=email-asian-american-solidarity-economies-co-op-housing-win-black-food-sovereignty-demands&email_referrer=email_823205&email_subject=in-defense-of-black-life-we-demand-community-control

^{lxxi} James Manyika, Susan Lund, Michael Chui, Jacques Bughin, Jonathan Woetzel, Parul Batra, Ryan Ko, and Saurabh, *Better Schools Won't Fix America.* 2019. https://www.theatlantic.com/magazine/archive/2019/07/education-isnt-enough/590611/?utm_source=The+Hechinger+Report&utm_campaign=6148284e9a-EMAIL_CAMPAIGN_WEEKLY_2019_06_18_03_04&utm_medium=email&utm_term=0_d3ee4c3e04-6148284e9a-322736177Sanghvi, *Jobs lost, jobs gained: What the future of work will mean for jobs, skills, and wages,* Mckinsey & Company. https://www.mckinsey.com/featured-insights/future-of-work/jobs-lost-jobs-gained-what-the-future-of-work-will-mean-for-jobs-skills-and-wages

^{lxxii} MIT, *MIT Open Courseware,* https://ocw.mit.edu/index.htm

^{lxxiii} *Graduation and retention rates,* WGU. https://www.wgu.edu/about/students-graduates/retention-graduation-rates.html

^{lxxiv} James Manyika, Susan Lund, Michael Chui, Jacques Bughin, Jonathan Woetzel, Parul Batra, Ryan Ko, and Saurabh Sanghvi, *Better Schools Won't Fix America.*

Jobs lost, jobs gained: What the future of work will mean for jobs, skills, and wages, Mckinsey & Company. https://www.mckinsey.com/featured-insights/future-of-work/jobs-lost-jobs-gained-what-the-future-of-work-will-mean-for-jobs-skills-and-wages

^{lxxv} Free online courses from Massachusetts Institute of Technology. Through MITx, the Institute furthers its commitment to improving education worldwide. MITx courses embody the inventiveness, openness, rigor and

quality that are hallmarks of MIT, and many use materials developed for MIT residential courses in the Institute's five schools and 33 academic disciplines. Courses can be audited free or students can choose to receive a verified   certificate   for   a   small   fee.

MIT, MITx Free online courses from Massachusetts Institute of Technology,

[lxxvi] Alicia Prince, *25 Killer Sites For Free Online Education,* lifehack.org. https://www.lifehack.org/articles/money/25-killer-sites-for-free-online-education.html

[lxxvii]   James Manyika, Susan Lund, Michael Chui, Jacques Bughin, Jonathan Woetzel, Parul Batra, Ryan Ko, and Saurabh, *Better Schools Won't Fix America.* https://www.theatlantic.com/magazine/archive/2019/07/education-isnt-enough/590611/?utm_source=The+Hechinger+Report&utm_campaign=6148284e9a-EMAIL_CAMPAIGN_WEEKLY_2019_06_18_03_04&utm_medium=email&utm_term=0_d3ee4c3e04-6148284e9a-322736177Sanghvi

[lxxviii]   Uncredited writer, *WHAT IS THE NATIONAL DEBT COSTING US?* 2018. The Peterson Foundation. https://www.pgpf.org/blog/2018/11/we-will-soon-be-spending-more-on-national-debt-interest-than-on-these-vital-programs

[lxxix] Maggie Fitzgerald, The CEOs of nearly 200 companies just said shareholder value is no longer their main objective. 2019. CNBC Markets. https://www.cnbc.com/2019/08/19/the-ceos-of-nearly-two-hundred-companies-say-shareholder-value-is-no-longer-their-main-objective.html

[lxxx] Joel Stein, *Millennials: The Me Me Me Generation.* 2013. TIME. https://time.com/247/millennials-the-me-me-me-generation/

www.ingramcontent.com/pod-product-compliance
Lightning Source LLC
Chambersburg PA
CBHW031429150726
47989CB00002B/870